YOUR DAILY
W.O.W.!

Words of Wisdom That Will Inspire, Energize, and Empower You Every Day

BY

MELISSA WEST

ISBN: 1493688855
ISBN 13: 9781493688852
Library of Congress Cataloging-in-Publication Data

To protect the privacy of those who have shared their stories with the author, some details and names
may have been changed.

The internet addresses, email addresses, and phone numbers in this book are accurate at the time
of publication. They are provided as a resource. Author does not endorse them or vouch for their
content or permanence.

Published in association with Kary Oberbrunner—Redeem the Day, P.O. Box 43 Powell, OH, 4065,
www.karyoberbrunner.com

"I have watched Melissa mentor and impact leaders for several years. I am confident that this book will encourage you to be all you can be."
    -- John C. Maxwell – NY Times Best Selling Author

"The only thing better than starting my day with Melissa's Daily WOW blog is having a book full of her words of wisdom right on my desk to read during my day when I need a WOW shot. Drink up from Melissa's wisdom and insights and your life will be enriched."
    -- Paul Martinelli, President of the John Maxwell Team.

"Melissa's passion comes pouring out through these pages. She empowers us to achieve success and fulfillment every single day of the year."
    - Scott Fay, author of Discover Your Sweet Spot

"*Your Daily W.O.W.* should be a part of every successful person's daily reading. It's exactly what one needs to take their day and year to the next level."
    -- King Pinyin, Author, Speaker, Direct Sales Expert

"Melissa's words of wisdom challenge us to expand our thinking on a daily basis to find greater meaning and purpose in every day circumstance."
    -- Inge Rock, Author and Teacher

"Invest the few minutes needed to daily digest Melissa's Words of Wisdom ... You too will discover the spiritual, mental and emotional nourishment that may just give you the needed WOW to take the next step, answer the next question, or give the needed energy for the day.
    -- Rick Krug, Team Dream World Wide, LLC

For Christopher West,
My husband and soulmate
Thanks for showing me how to live with a standard of excellence

And for my Daily W.O.W. Readers,
This never would have become my first book without your encouragement
Thank you

ACKNOWLEDGEMENTS

Every day I feel so blessed and grateful for the life experiences and people that have been a part of my journey. I know I would not be where I am today if it wasn't for those experiences and people. Thank you!

I would like to acknowledge the mentors in my life who have really left their mark. These people have been my greatest teachers, supporters, encouragers, and friends:

My husband and best friend, Christopher West

My greatest mentors and teachers, Paul Martinelli, John C. Maxwell, and Anthony Robbins

My dear friend and coach, Kelly Sylte

My sister, Patty and Mom and Dad

They have all taught me so much of what I know today about business, life, and myself. They supported and encouraged me through the good times and bad. And they extended their hand of lifelong friendship. For that, I am forever grateful.

I would also like to acknowledge those who contributed to the making of this book. You were there to help me manage this project, brainstorm ideas, proofread, edit, and encourage me every step of the way. Thank you to Kary Oberbrunner, Stacey Shanahan, Alice Osborn, Fred Ford, and Tracey Gritz.

And of course I want to acknowledge all my Daily W.O.W. (Words of Wisdom) readers. This never would have become my first book without your encouragement. Thank you.

TABLE OF CONTENTS

Introduction:

THE SECRET POWER OF THE TAMBOURINE SHAKE!

They say confession is good for the soul. Based on this conventional wisdom, I thought I'd start my first book by admitting my addiction.

It's OK if you laugh. I think it's kinda funny too. Those who know me best know how much enthusiasm I have for life. It tends to ooze right out of me. A few months ago, I was facilitating a training call for the John Maxwell Mentorship Program. Our topic was an important one—the Power of Celebration.

A few callers chimed in and revealed specific ways how they celebrate. One technique in particular caught my attention. A woman named Chandler Peterson shared that she kept a tambourine in her car. Evidently she shakes it whenever she's stuck in the car for a long drive.

I thought to myself, "I WANT A TAMBOURINE!" I immediately went to Amazon and bought my first tambourine—red, of course, since it's my favorite color.

A few days later, my coveted tambourine finally arrived! I had no clue how much joy this little instrument infused into my life. It took celebration to a whole new level.

I learned that you can't shake a tambourine without it putting a smile on your face! Maybe a little silly, but still a powerful truth nonetheless.

This little noisemaker quickly multiplied. Soon I had four of them spread throughout the house. They helped position me into my peak state by shaking off (no pun intended) negativity, stress, and frustration.

Simply put, these little instruments function as my secret weapon and keep me poised for progress! Now every time I travel and speak, you bet I pack my tambourine.

But tambourines aren't my only secret weapon

You see, not too many years ago, I worked a 9 to 5 job. In that environment, I hit a wall and desperately needed a strong dose of energy, inspiration, and empowerment.

Providentially, I stumbled upon personal and professional growth. When I discovered this topic I also discovered my bliss.

I grew especially fond of personal development quotes. When I read them I felt energized and inspired. Unable to keep quiet, I shared them occasionally, with friends and colleagues. Eventually, I started adding my own commentary. Turns out other people needed a daily dose of energy, inspiration, and empowerment, too.

My shift from 9 to 5 Web Administrator to full time Life and Business Success Coach, required me to operate on an entirely new level. These daily quotes enabled me to achieve that elevation.

Years later when I bought that first red tambourine, I felt a similar feeling; energized, inspired, and empowered.

Let's be honest though. Not everyone wants to fill their houses with tambourines. Because of this fact, I thought I'd design a book that offers a similar payoff. You hold in your hands a tool that will energize, inspire, and empower you to reach your next level. Each page of this book has been thoughtfully crafted with that goal in mind.

Take a peek at the structure and see what I mean:

JANUARY 1ˢᵀ

Ready to Make a Change?

A quote to energize you

"If you don't change the direction you are going, then you're likely to end up where you are heading."
~ John C. Maxwell

Words of Wisdom to inspire you

Have you identified the things in your life that you would like to change, but you keep finding yourself saying that "someday" you will do something about it? If you have a case of the "somedays" I hate to say it, but you are just moving further away from your desired destination. When you keep doing what you're doing, guess what, you will keep getting what you're getting. Don't complain or be frustrated if you are headed in the wrong direction, because you will continue to end up there until you make the decision to honor your greater self, do something about it and change directions. Listen to that voice deep within you that tells you "You can do it ... Go for it ... You've waited long enough."

Empowered to A.C.T.:

A call to action to empower you

What inspired **ACTION** will you take today?
What purposeful **CHANGE** will you make today?
What can you **TEACH** someone else today?

Happy Heading into a NEW and EMPOWERING Direction!

Remember, nothing happens until you decide to take action!

My hope is that you'll read one Daily W.O.W. per day for the next 365 days. If you do, it will help you feel energized, inspired and empowered to create an even more amazing life, without the need for a tambourine. Remember, success begins with the way you start your day. Start yours with a Daily W.O.W.

Happy Travels as you Enjoy the Secret Power of Quotes (or Tambourines if you prefer)!

January

Ready to Make a Change?

"If you don't change the direction you are going,
then you're likely to end up where you are heading."
~ John C. Maxwell

Have you identified the things in your life that you would like to change, but you keep finding yourself saying that "someday" you will do something about it? If you have a case of the "somedays" I hate to say it, but you are just moving further away from your desired destination. When you keep doing what you're doing you will keep getting what you're getting. Don't complain or be frustrated if you are headed in the wrong direction, because you will continue to end up there until you make the decision to honor your greater self, do something about it and change your direction. Listen to that voice deep within you that says, "You can do it ... Go for it ... You've waited long enough."

—◦ Empowered to A.C.T.: ◦—

What inspired **ACTION** will you take today?
What purposeful **CHANGE** will you make today?
What can you **TEACH** someone else today?

Happy Heading in a NEW and EMPOWERING Direction!

Remember, nothing happens until you decide to take action!

Work Your Magic Universe!

"When you want something, all the universe conspires
in helping you to achieve it."
~ Paulo Coelho

Many people think the world is out to get them. They think they are a victim of their circumstances and they feel stuck in a "woe is me" pity party. The truth of the matter is that God (some may prefer to use the word Universe) wants nothing more than for you to be a vibrant and full expression of your true self. Why on earth would God want to hold you back? You have a great purpose for being on this planet and God conspires to put people, situations, and experiences in your pathway so that you can live out your greatest and highest good. The thing is it is up to YOU whether you open or close the door to those people, situations, and experiences.

⟶ Empowered to A.C.T.: ⟵

What inspired **ACTION** will you take today?
What purposeful **CHANGE** will you make today?
What can you **TEACH** someone else today?

Happy Allowing God to Work its Magic!

Remember, nothing happens until you decide to take action!

Find Your Truth

"To find yourself, think for yourself."
~ Socrates

At a very young age, children are conditioned to depend on others to tell them who and what they are. They're taught what's right and wrong, beautiful and ugly, acceptable and unacceptable. Before you know it, that child is programmed and operating according to what everyone else believes about them. They're seeking to please and gain approval of others while abandoning their true and authentic selves. Take a moment today and look beyond what you've been taught about yourself and who you are. Take a deeper look inside yourself and reflect upon what you see and feel. That's where your truth is. It's not outside of you, but rather it's on the inside!

— Empowered to A.C.T.: —

What inspired **ACTION** will you take today?
What purposeful **CHANGE** will you make today?
What can you **TEACH** someone else today?

Happy Finding Your Truth!

Remember, nothing happens until you decide to take action!

Today's Featured Reader:
Stacy Krafczyk, Milwaukee, Wisconsin
"This is a life-changing quote that helped me look inside myself before looking to others for attention. Your words of wisdom are SO empowering because we look outside of ourselves for approval, attention and love all the time. But if we begin to look within ourselves FIRST, we wouldn't be let down, feel lonely, sad or isolated because we would find our true happiness within first! I've learned that true happiness and love begins from within! Thank you Melissa for being a part of my life's journey!"

Your Once in a Lifetime Moment!

"EVERY experience is a once in a lifetime experience."
~ Unknown

Stop for a moment and see the significance and power in this present moment. You will never ever have this exact same moment back ... ever. It truly is a once in a lifetime moment! WOW, how cool is that? What will you do with it? Who will you meet? Where will you go? Even though it may appear that you are experiencing the same things over and over some days, recognize that the choice to be open to something new is always available for you in this present moment. You can open yourself up to new opportunities, new relationships, new conversations, new ideas, etc. or you can assume that you know exactly how the experience will turn out and miss out on any new gifts that always come in the present moment.

⟶ Empowered to A.C.T.: ⟵

What inspired **ACTION** will you take today?
What purposeful **CHANGE** will you make today?
What can you **TEACH** someone else today?

Happy Once In a Lifetime Moments!

Remember, nothing happens until you decide to take action!

Set Yourself Apart from Mediocrity!

"In a sea of mediocrity, just knowing what you want to do and then making an effort to pursue it distinguishes you from almost everybody."
~ John C. Maxwell

Many people scratch their heads and don't understand why they are unable to achieve excellence in their lives. Most of these people are not crystal clear on what they want. If you don't know what you really want, then how do you know where to put your time, energy, and effort? I have a Post-it I keep on my laptop that says, "Get Clear." It is a constant reminder to me to be very clear on what my intention is and what I really want to create and experience in my life. It takes a lot of the guesswork out of making decisions and knowing what and where to go next. Set yourself apart. Get clear and then take action on what your heart has a clear, burning desire for!

Empowered to A.C.T.:

What inspired **ACTION** will you take today?
What purposeful **CHANGE** will you make today?
What can you **TEACH** someone else today?

Happy Setting Yourself Apart From Mediocrity!

Remember, nothing happens until you decide to take action!

Bless Everyone!

"If you want to be blessed with all the good things in life, learn to silently bless everyone with all the good things in life."
~ Deepak Chopra

Whatever it is that you seek in your life, seek first to bless others with it. Maybe you seek more joy and happiness in your days, more positive energy, passion and good fortune. If that's the case, learn to share those things with others. Be that person who openly shares their joy and passion. Be that person who oozes positive energy! Be that person who helps others earn a good fortune. Be that person who says a silent prayer for those in need. By doing so, all these wonderful things are granted to you as well. Who will you bless today? And what will you bless them with?

⸻ Empowered to A.C.T.: ⸻

What inspired **ACTION** will you take today?
What purposeful **CHANGE** will you make today?
What can you **TEACH** someone else today?

Happy Blessing Others!

Remember, nothing happens until you decide to take action!

You Are Amazing!

"… and when you smile, the whole world stops and stares for a while…
'Cause, girl, you're amazing just the way you are …"
~ Bruno Mars

This is one of those songs I can listen to over and over. Bruno Mars came out with his song, "Just the Way You Are" a few years ago and every time I hear it, it still puts a smile on my face. It reminds me to stop and just love myself exactly where I am in my life, here and now. So often we get caught up in trying so hard to be SOMEBODY else and be SOMEWHERE else in our lives that we miss out on enjoying and LOVING ourselves here and now. Stop and recognize there is soooo much to love about yourself, right here and right now!

Empowered to A.C.T.:

What inspired **ACTION** will you take today?
What purposeful **CHANGE** will you make today?
What can you **TEACH** someone else today?

Happy Loving Yourself Just the Way You Are!

Remember, nothing happens until you decide to take action!

Your Perception is Your Reality!

"When you change the way you look at things,
the things you look at change."
~ Dr. Wayne Dyer

Dr. Wayne Dyer is one of my all-time favorite authors and this is one of my favorite quotes by him. I invite you to challenge yourself to see things differently, to alter your perception, your point of view, on a regular basis. See if you are able to shift your perception to a point where you look at a situation/person differently than you usually do. Look for the magnificence and beauty. Look for the lesson and opportunity. Look for the real message ... the insight and wisdom. I guarantee you it is there; you just have to be willing to look closer.

⸺ Empowered to A.C.T.: ⸺

What inspired **ACTION** will you take today?
What purposeful **CHANGE** will you make today?
What can you **TEACH** someone else today?

Happy New Perceptions!

Remember, nothing happens until you decide to take action!

What is in Your Heart?

"I have never thought of writing for the reputation and honor. What I have in my heart must come out; that is the reason why I compose."
~ Ludwig Van Beethoven

After reading this quote, it really reminded me how much I love writing these Daily W.O.W.'s and how each of these daily messages come straight from my heart. I really enjoy writing them and I can't stop writing them! They have become a part of not just my business, but they have become a part of ME! I realize now that by writing these I am allowing my life's purpose to flow through me. I am letting what is in my heart flow out through the words I write. I thank you for being a part of my life's purpose and for allowing me to share a part of my heart with you every day. Now what is in your heart that must flow out? How can you express more of what's in your heart today?

⁓ Empowered to A.C.T: ⁓

What inspired **ACTION** will you take today?
What purposeful **CHANGE** will you make today?
What can you **TEACH** someone else today?

Happy Expressing What's In Your Heart!

Remember, nothing happens until you decide to take action!

I Challenge You to Walk Your Talk

"I challenge you to make your life a masterpiece. I challenge you to join the ranks of those people who live what they teach, who walk their talk."
~ Anthony Robbins

Do you walk your talk? So many people can talk big and say they know what they want in life; however, when it comes down to taking responsibility for creating these big dreams in their life, they fall short. I am such a strong believer in walking your talk and then teaching and mentoring others by talking your walk. Who do you need to be in order to walk your talk? It doesn't mean you have to be perfect, it doesn't mean you get it right every time, it doesn't mean you never fall short of your goal—what it does mean is that you are living your life in alignment to what you say you want and who you say you want to be. It means you are true and impeccable with your word while you are actively taking action with it.

—⚬ Empowered to A.C.T.: ⚬—

What inspired **ACTION** will you take today?
What purposeful **CHANGE** will you make today?
What can you **TEACH** someone else today?

Happy Walking Your Talk ... and then Talking Your Walk!

Remember, nothing happens until you decide to take action!

You Are Unique!

"No two men are just alike. Every new life is a new thing under the sun; there has
never been anything like it before, and never will be again."
~ Henry Ford

You have a unique gift! And that is YOU being YOU! There is not another "You"
on this planet, nor will there ever be in the history of mankind. You are special in
your own way. The key is to find your uniqueness and express and share it with
the world! The world is starving for you to do so! The society we live in tries to
get us to conform and be the same; however, it is our job to discover our unique
gifts and talents and develop them in a way that will serve humanity to make this
beautiful planet we live on an even better place! You being YOU is the best way
to achieve that! Take this moment to write out three things that make you unique
and special.

⸺ Empowered to A.C.T.: ⸺

What inspired **ACTION** will you take today?
What purposeful **CHANGE** will you make today?
What can you **TEACH** someone else today?

Happy Being Uniquely YOU!

Remember, nothing happens until you decide to take action!

What Do Your Circumstances Tell You?

"Circumstance does not make the man; it reveals him to himself."
~ James Allen

This is a great quote because it requires you be real honest in order to gain true insight about yourself. You see, the circumstances in your life are there to show you more of who you are being. Angry people get angry toward their circumstances, drama kings and queens are dramatic toward their circumstances, loving and kind people are loving and kind toward their circumstances. The circumstance itself doesn't matter so much as how you respond to it. Take a look at your responses to your life's circumstances. Your life is a mirror. It is revealing how you are and who you are being.

Empowered to A.C.T.:

What inspired **ACTION** will you take today?
What purposeful **CHANGE** will you make today?
What can you **TEACH** someone else today?

Happy Insight!

Remember, nothing happens until you decide to take action!

You Must Experience It to Know It!

"If you know, yet do not do, you do not know."
~ Oie Osterkamp

This quote hits close to home as a life/business coach and trainer because often I hear people say, "Yeah, yeah, I know this stuff already." However, they are not applying it and living it. There's big talk, but no walk. They may know it at an intellectual level, but they do not know it at an experiential level, which makes a HUGE difference! What are you claiming to know, yet have not done much work to fully experience and master this knowing? In other words, where do you have a big talk, but no walk? Many folks know what they should be doing to reach their goal and achieve mastery, but they are not doing much about it, even though it's what they say they want and who they say they want to be.

Empowered to A.C.T.:

What inspired **ACTION** will you take today?
What purposeful **CHANGE** will you make today?
What can you **TEACH** someone else today?

Happy Closing the Gap Between Knowing and Doing!

Remember, nothing happens until you decide to take action!

Choose What Motivates You!

"Be miserable. Or motivate yourself. Whatever has to be done,
it's always your choice!"
~ Wayne Dyer

I love that you and I have a choice every morning, day, and night as to how we want to live the days of our lives. We can choose to be motivated by love and passion or we can choose to drown ourselves in fear and misery. We can choose to walk around with a smile on our faces or a frown. We can choose to be distant and cold with people or we can choose to be connected and warm with people. For me, I try to choose love and passion as much as I can. I let it drive me. I am unstoppable and my willingness to do whatever it takes INCREASES! You see, it's all a choice, my friends! What will you choose today?

⚬ Empowered to A.C.T.: ⚬

What inspired **ACTION** will you take today?
What purposeful **CHANGE** will you make today?
What can you **TEACH** someone else today?

Happy Choosing to Be Motivated by Love and Passion!

Remember, nothing happens until you decide to take action!

BE Your Message!

"Any message you try and convey must contain a piece of you. You can't just deliver words. You can't merely convey information. You need to be more than just a messenger. You must be the message you want to deliver."
~ John C. Maxwell

Whenever you are sharing a message with others, be sure you first connect with and live out the message on a personal and emotional level even before you share it. How can you expect others to connect to it and live it if you yourself are not connected to it? You must internalize it and "make it your own" so that when you speak, you are being your message from your heart and experiences, and people will instantly see your authenticity and credibility. That is when others are truly inspired by your message! Have you ever been inspired by someone who wasn't connected to their own message? NOPE, didn't think so! CONNECT with your message, BE your message, and SHARE your message!

⟿ Empowered to A.C.T.: ⟿

What inspired **ACTION** will you take today?
What purposeful **CHANGE** will you make today?
What can you **TEACH** someone else today?

Happy Connecting, Being, and Sharing Your Message!

Remember, nothing happens until you decide to take action!

Today's Featured Reader:
Eric Hermans, Belguim
"Your words touch me, Melissa! I love your daily words! Thank you!"

Where Are You?

"I know I am right where I am supposed to be."
~ Danny Archer

What if you are exactly where you are supposed to be? LET GO of the idea that you aren't. Regardless of whether you are dealing with an obstacle, setback, disappointment, or a great success! It doesn't matter if you are in a peak or a valley, you are supposed to be there to learn and grow from that exact experience. It's funny because if we are doing great and achieving big successes, we believe we are supposed to be there. However, when we have a setback and disappointment, we don't believe we should have to go through that experience. What if ALL experiences were purposeful? I believe they are and I invite you to believe the same. It will serve you during tough times and it will be easier to let go of the resistance to see the lesson before you.

— Empowered to A.C.T.: —

What inspired **ACTION** will you take today?
What purposeful **CHANGE** will you make today?
What can you **TEACH** someone else today?

Happy Being Right Where You Are!

Remember, nothing happens until you decide to take action!

True Success Comes From Your Heart!

"True success comes from the passion in your heart, not your mind. Your mind will chase a paycheck. Your heart will seek to fulfill your purpose."
~ Melissa West (Malueg)

As I began my journey of revealing my purpose to myself, I discovered that true success is about creating your heart's desire, not your mind's desire. The mind will chase a paycheck, while the heart is looking to fulfill your purpose and calling and make a difference in this world. I am sure you would agree that when your heart is in it, whether it's a project you're working on, parenting, or a relationship, that you are more resourceful, creative, energetic, and passionate than when you're just stuck in your head and your mind is racing all over the place! Don't get me wrong, the intellectual mind is an amazing and powerful instrument, but realize that it is meant to SERVE what lives in your heart. Let your heart guide you and allow your mind to be in service of your heart's desires!

—◦ Empowered to A.C.T.: ◦—

What inspired **ACTION** will you take today?
What purposeful **CHANGE** will you make today?
What can you **TEACH** someone else today?

Happy Creating Your Heart's Desire!

Remember, nothing happens until you decide to take action!

Live With Love, Grace, and Gratitude!

"Happiness cannot be traveled to, owned, earned, worn, or consumed. Happiness is the spiritual experience of living every minute with love, grace, and gratitude."
~ Denis Waitley

Happiness is in your heart and soul! It's always there and always has been and always will be. Don't seek happiness outside of you; it's not there. Don't look for it in a job, a vacation, a nice car, or a nice home. When you create an attachment of your happiness to things, if they are taken away from you, then so too goes your happiness. Find happiness within your heart and seek to express it. When you express the love, grace, and gratitude in your heart at all times, no matter what, you will be happy! I guarantee it!

─◦ Empowered to A.C.T.: ◦─

What inspired **ACTION** will you take today?
What purposeful **CHANGE** will you make today?
What can you **TEACH** someone else today?

Happy Expressing Your Happiness!

Remember, nothing happens until you decide to take action!

Family is a Slice of Heaven

"A happy family is but an earlier heaven."
~ George Bernard Shaw

When you and your family are happy, it can feel like a slice of heaven! There is a connection and a closeness that words can't even describe. Make your time with your family a priority that is meaningful, because when you do it will feel like heaven. Just over four years ago now (wow, time flies!), I decided to move closer to my family and I am now blessed to live just a short 25 minutes from my sister and her family. My parents just recently moved back to the U.S. after living in Brazil for the last eight years. They are now just 10 minutes down the road. I love the time we get to now spend together! Know this too that family isn't just your biological family. Families are the people who love you for you and are there for you when you need them most. My "family" goes far beyond just my biological family! I believe yours does too!

⌁ Empowered to A.C.T.: ⌁

What inspired **ACTION** will you take today?
What purposeful **CHANGE** will you make today?
What can you **TEACH** someone else today?

Happy Family!

Remember, nothing happens until you decide to take action!

Live in Abundance

"Like the air you breathe, abundance in all things is available to you. Your life will simply be as good as you allow it to be."
~ Esther Hicks (From the Teachings of Abraham)

Ahhhh, take a nice deep cleansing breath! Stop and think for a moment ... before you took that breath, did you think to yourself, "Geez, I sure hope there's enough oxygen for me." Or did you think, "I better not take too deep of a breath or there might not be enough for everyone else." I'm going to guess that neither of those thoughts came to mind! Why? Because we know there's an abundance of air, more than enough for all of us. Do you think that same way when it comes to money? How about possibilities? Why not? Most of us have been conditioned to believe there are limited answers, limited resources, and you aren't deserving of abundance. The more abundance you allow into your life, the more will come with ease, which in turn will allow you to serve at greater levels! It's up to you to relate the abundance of the air you breathe to everything else in this world. Think and feel in abundance and you will live in abundance!

—⚬ Empowered to A.C.T.: ⚬—

What inspired **ACTION** will you take today?
What purposeful **CHANGE** will you make today?
What can you **TEACH** someone else today?

Happy Abundance Everywhere!

Remember, nothing happens until you decide to take action!

Follow Your Heart!

"There are many things that will catch my eye, but there are only a few that catch my heart. It is those I consider to pursue."
~ Tim Redmond

It can be easy to place your awareness on what everyone else is doing and accomplishing; however, that does not mean that is what you are supposed to go do with your life now. Before you make any goal-setting decisions, you must check in with your heart and see what it is thinking, feeling, saying to you. Are you being guided by your heart or your head? I guarantee you this, those endeavors that catch your heart will be more fulfilling and longer lasting than anything that merely catches your eye and ego. Listen to your heart. What is it telling you?

⌐ Empowered to A.C.T.: ¬

What inspired **ACTION** will you take today?
What purposeful **CHANGE** will you make today?
What can you **TEACH** someone else today?

Happy Following Your Heart!

Remember, nothing happens until you decide to take action!

Experience Life's Lessons!

"Life is a succession of lessons which must be lived to be understood."
~ Ralph Waldo Emerson

Wouldn't it be nice if you could become the successful person you intend to be so you could bypass the lessons? On the surface that sounds nice, but the lessons are life's gifts that cannot be understood and fully received unless they are experienced first-hand. You cannot become that which you never experience. True growth comes from living your life and experiencing all that life has to offer. Take a look at what you are experiencing right now and give thanks for the gift of life; give thanks that you get to learn and grow through life's abundance of lessons!

— Empowered to A.C.T.: —

What inspired **ACTION** will you take today?
What purposeful **CHANGE** will you make today?
What can you **TEACH** someone else today?

Happy Living Life's Lessons!

Remember, nothing happens until you decide to take action!

Reach, Stretch, and Grow

"Life without progress becomes unendurable, and the person who ceases from growth must either become an imbecile or insane. The greater and more harmonious and well-rounded your growth is, the happier you will be."
~ Wallace D. Wattles

There is no such thing as standing still and not growing. It really comes down to one important question you must ask yourself: am I GROWING or DYING? Everything is either in a state of development or a state of disintegration. You are either moving forward or moving backward. There is no standing still. Therefore, it is imperative that you consciously and deliberately develop yourself emotionally, intellectually, and spiritually on a consistent basis. It's actually your spiritual nature you want to expand and express yourself in greater ways. When you are not progressing in life, you are cutting off and denying your spirit the joy of expansion and expression. In every moment there is an opportunity to express yourself authentically and purposefully. Take advantage of it … your happiness and fulfillment depend on it!

⸺ Empowered to A.C.T.: ⸺

What inspired **ACTION** will you take today?
What purposeful **CHANGE** will you make today?
What can you **TEACH** someone else today?

Happy Expression and Expansion of Your Greatest Self!

Remember, nothing happens until you decide to take action!

What Do You Focus On?

"Companies that solely focus on competition will ultimately die. Those that focus on value creation will thrive."

~ Edward de Bano

You do not need to own a company in order to add value to your life and others' lives. You see, YOU ARE the CEO of your own life! Where you place your focus matters! Are you focused on competing with others or with adding value to the world? You must ask yourself, "What value am I creating in my own life and in the life of others?" Notice that an intention to just outdo someone else will only get you so far. You will always have your eye on the other person and you will never truly live a valuable life. Have the intention to bring true value into the lives of those you are serving— your life will thrive beyond your wildest dreams.

— Empowered to A.C.T.: —

What inspired **ACTION** will you take today?
What purposeful **CHANGE** will you make today?
What can you **TEACH** someone else today?

Happy Creating Value!

Remember, nothing happens until you decide to take action!

Be Decisive and Take Action!

"Successful people make bold decisions and they follow through on them."
~ Unknown

It's one thing to be decisive—it's another thing to be fully committed to your decisions and actually follow through with action. Those who are massively successful are fully committed to their decisions. They are decisive and they back up their decisions with ACTION! Are you fully committed to your decisions? In order to move forward and create more success in your life, you must be really honest with yourself when answering that question. There's no sense in telling yourself just what you want to hear! Be honest and then be willing to work on and develop your ability to make sound decisions and increase your commitment level to taking action. This may take time, so be gentle on yourself as well!

⟶ Empowered to A.C.T.: ⟵

What inspired **ACTION** will you take today?
What purposeful **CHANGE** will you make today?
What can you **TEACH** someone else today?

Happy Making Decisions and Taking Action!

Remember, nothing happens until you decide to take action!

Are You Smiling Yet?

"Don't be weighed down by things that drain your energy! If it doesn't bring you
joy chuck it, change it, or rearrange it!"
~ Ralph Waldo Emerson

Great questions I like to ask myself frequently about the things I do, places I go,
and people I hang out with are, "Am I lifted up or drained … Am I energized or
dragged down … Am I inspired or frustrated?" The answers to these questions
really help me make decisions as to where and with whom I spend my time. You
never get a minute back … the power is always in this present moment. Choose to
be in environments and around people who lift you up, energize you, and inspire
you! Just by making this a part of your decision-making process, you will open
yourself up to receiving greater energy, joy and bliss into your life!

—◦ Empowered to A.C.T.: ◦—

What inspired **ACTION** will you take today?
What purposeful **CHANGE** will you make today?
What can you **TEACH** someone else today?

Happy Being Lifted Up, Energized, and Inspired!

Remember, nothing happens until you decide to take action!

Turn Your Life Around

"With a greater awareness, anyone can turn their life around."
~ Paul Martinelli

I remember when I started studying human potential and development. I was amazed to find out what we human beings are truly capable of! It was like I was in the dark and someone turned the light on! As you widen your self-awareness, you open yourself up to a whole new level of thinking and more of your true self awakens and emerges. When that happens, you see yourself and your world differently and you begin to naturally take the necessary action to change your life to live a more authentic and true life. What are you plugged into on a regular basis that causes you to widen your self-awareness? In other words, what helps you break free from small and limited thinking?

— Empowered to A.C.T.: —

What inspired **ACTION** will you take today?
What purposeful **CHANGE** will you make today?
What can you **TEACH** someone else today?

Happy Changing Your Life with Greater Self-Awareness!

Remember, nothing happens until you decide to take action!

Live Your Dream Now!

"If you were living the life of your dreams right now,
would you act any differently?"
~ David Dove

One of my favorite things to say is "Live the Dream!" So if you were actually living the life of your dreams right now, what would be different about you? What would you be doing? How would you show up differently? What would you be saying? Who would you be talking to? How would you be standing? What would you be thinking about? Paint the picture in your mind of all that you would be thinking, saying, and how your physiology would look like. Why wait until your dreams come true for you to become this person? No time like the present. BE that person here and now! Practice thinking what that person thinks, saying what that person says, standing like that person stands. The power is always in the present moment! Live your dreams right here and right now!

⸺ Empowered to A.C.T.: ⸺

What inspired **ACTION** will you take today?
What purposeful **CHANGE** will you make today?
What can you **TEACH** someone else today?

Happy Living the Dream, My Friend!

Remember, nothing happens until you decide to take action!

What Ladder Are You Climbing?

"As you climb the ladder of success, be sure it's
leaning against the right building."
~ Jackson Brown Jr.

Sometimes we work really hard to work our way up the ladder just to find out
we're climbing the wrong ladder! Have you ever done that? Maybe it's a college
degree or job ... maybe it's a relationship. Whatever it is, you realize one day that
you're not on the ladder you really want to be on. Take a moment to do a self-
inventory and see if you are putting your precious time and energy into what your
heart REALLY has a burning desire for! Simply ask yourself, "Is this moving me
toward what I really want in my life? What my heart and soul seeks and longs for?
Do I have a burning desire to create this in my life?" Listen for the answers and
then be true to your heart.

— Empowered to A.C.T.:

What inspired **ACTION** will you take today?
What purposeful **CHANGE** will you make today?
What can you **TEACH** someone else today?

Happy Climbing the Right Ladder!

Remember, nothing happens until you decide to take action!

Have You Expressed Gratitude Today Yet?

"Silent gratitude isn't much use to anyone."
~ G.B. Stern

Who and what are you grateful for? Have you expressed that gratitude lately? If yes, keep it up because it's so powerful and makes such a significant and positive impact in yours and others' lives. If not, then the time is NOW! There's no reason to keep gratitude to yourself ... EXPRESS IT! Make a list of people and things you are grateful for and share this gratitude. The more you do this, the more you significantly lift others and yourself up! I am grateful to YOU for reading this today and choosing to do something with it! YOU inspire me!

—◦ Empowered to A.C.T.: ◦—

What inspired **ACTION** will you take today?
What purposeful **CHANGE** will you make today?
What can you **TEACH** someone else today?

Happy Expressing Gratitude!

Remember, nothing happens until you decide to take action!

Anger Makes You Smaller

"Anger makes you smaller, while forgiveness forces you
to grow beyond what you were."
~ Cherie Carter-Scott

It's not always easy and it can actually be quite difficult to release feelings of anger
and forgive others as well as forgive ourselves! Realize that the act of forgiveness is
actually part of your growth and evolution; it's transformational. It enhances who
you are. When you forgive you are choosing to express a higher side of yourself.
Instead of harboring anger toward someone and expressing it toward them, find
the love in your heart to choose to say a prayer and bless those who anger you and
then let it go. It is doing you no good to hold onto it. You don't evolve into the
person you want to be through anger; it's only through love, my friends!

─○ Empowered to A.C.T.: ○─

What inspired **ACTION** will you take today?
What purposeful **CHANGE** will you make today?
What can you **TEACH** someone else today?

Happy Evolving Through Love!

Remember, nothing happens until you decide to take action!

February

Read Great Books!

"There are worse crimes than burning books.
One of them is not reading them."
~ Joseph Brodsky

I love to read great books! I am constantly inspired by clever words and memorable phrases! I get inspired when I can internalize what I'm reading and I especially love it when I can then go out and create something new and purposeful from something I've read. If you are looking to learn, grow, and make a positive change in your life, then you MUST feed your mind and heart something that will expand your awareness of life as you know it. Be sure you are fueling your mind and heart with great books that cause you to reach, stretch, and grow!

Empowered to A.C.T.:

What inspired **ACTION** will you take today?
What purposeful **CHANGE** will you make today?
What can you **TEACH** someone else today?

Happy Growing Through Reading!

Remember, nothing happens until you decide to take action!

Live With Purpose!

You'll find that with a clear Life Purpose, you'll look for purpose behind
every activity, and if you don't see how it fits into your purpose,
you'll naturally choose to do something that does. Everything
you do should be an expression of your Life Purpose.
~ Jack Canfield

I am a purpose junkie! I love love love finding a greater meaning behind everything
that I do! I love seeing how my choices are an expression of what has been placed in
my heart and soul. I love living out my true calling! How about you? Are you in love
with your Life's Purpose? I believe you have to fall in love with your Life's Purpose
before you will actually let it become the compass of your life. I wake up every
morning and believe that I have been given the best Life Purpose on the planet and
am so grateful and honored to live it out. How about you? Do you love living out
your Life's Purpose or hiding from your true calling? The time is NOW, my friends!
Choose to live your every waking moment with great purpose and meaning! What's
one thing you can do to live more purposefully today?

Empowered to A.C.T.:

What inspired **ACTION** will you take today?
What purposeful **CHANGE** will you make today?
What can you **TEACH** someone else today?

Happy Living Your Life Purpose!

Remember, nothing happens until you decide to take action!

Make Others Feel Valued!

"The key to making others feel valued in a group or on a team is to invite participation. The smartest person in the room is never as smart as all the people in the room. Input creates synergy, buy-in, and connection."
~ John C. Maxwell

It makes so much sense, doesn't it?! When you're not being asked to participate, it can be easy to feel like you're not adding value to the team. Because if you were adding value, then they would be asking for your participation. By simply asking for everyone to participate, you immediately give each person a sense of value. Go into your day today making others feel more valued. And when you do, there will be an opportunity for your team to connect at even greater levels! Nothing really compares to the powerful ideas, synergy, and relationships that come from a powerful and effective team. Think about the last time you had a really effective brainstorming session with other like-minded individuals ... Powerful, isn't it? But before you can create that kind of synergy and outcome, you must invite everyone's participation and make everyone feel valued. When people feel valued, they are much more passionate and willing to get involved and contribute their greatest ideas and skillsets to the team.

Empowered to A.C.T.:

What inspired **ACTION** will you take today?
What purposeful **CHANGE** will you make today?
What can you **TEACH** someone else today?

Happy Making Others Feel Valued!

Remember, nothing happens until you decide to take action!

Be Honest AND Impeccable!

"Honesty doesn't have to be brutal, but it has to be honest."
~ Simon Sinek

Have you ever had someone be brutally honest with you? Would have liked the honesty minus the brutality? Take a moment and think about how you communicate. Think about how you can be honest AND be impeccable with your word at the same time while leaving out the brutality. Think about how differently you will communicate as well as how differently your message could be received! Communication is everything! Everyone on this planet communicates all day, every day in various forms. It is important to develop and master your ability to communicate with honesty and impeccability! How can you make this the foundation for how you communicate?

⚬ Empowered to A.C.T.: ⚬

What inspired **ACTION** will you take today?
What purposeful **CHANGE** will you make today?
What can you **TEACH** someone else today?

Happy Being Honest and Impeccable!

Remember, nothing happens until you decide to take action!

You Are the Greatest!

"I am the greatest. I said that even before I knew I was."
~ Muhammad Ali

Most people wait for the end results in their life to tell them how great they are. I invite you to entertain the thought that regardless of the results you have in your life today, you are GREAT! The time is here and now to claim your greatness, my friend! Whatever results you are seeking to create in your life, you must begin to recognize your ability and power to create them. You must see the great power within you! Each and every one of us has a greatness that the world is waiting for us to express. Unfortunately, many people harbor and suppress their greatness and never live fully into and from it. Don't rob yourself of experiencing and living your greatness.

Empowered to A.C.T.:

What inspired **ACTION** will you take today?
What purposeful **CHANGE** will you make today?
What can you **TEACH** someone else today?

Happy Greatness!

Remember, nothing happens until you decide to take action!

Take Inspired Action

"Take action out of inspiration, not desperation."
~ Unknown

Think about the huge difference it makes when you take action from a place of inspiration rather than desperation. Think about it ... It's huge, isn't it? When you are going through your day acting out of inspiration you have more energy, more zest, and more passion for everything you do. You are more likely to give your best and put your heart and soul into it. When you act out of desperation things get ugly real fast. You most likely come from a place of fear and lack and so therefore everything you experience loses its intended beauty and you aren't able to pick up the gifts and lessons along the way. As a result you will miss out greatly. Choose to connect to your Source and Creator today and ignite the inspiration within you! Be guided by your spirit!

─◦ Empowered to A.C.T.: ◦─

What inspired **ACTION** will you take today?
What purposeful **CHANGE** will you make today?
What can you **TEACH** someone else today?

Happy Inspired Action!

Remember, nothing happens until you decide to take action!

What If ...?

*"The greatest mistake you can make in life is to be
continually fearing you will make one."*
~ Elbert Hubbard

Do you ever get caught up in a fearful "What if ...?" thought process? You might think, "What if this doesn't work out the way I planned ... What if this is a mistake ... What if I fail?" Well, that worrying and fearing the worst case scenario actually causes unnecessary stress and anxiety and can actually paralyze you from moving forward and taking action! Instead, ask a better question. Ask, "What if I learn something new from this experience no matter how it turns out ... What if I learn something about myself and it actually makes me stronger ... What if it DOES turn out exactly how I planned ...?" Recognize the power in the questions you ask yourself. They can either lead to more fear or more empowerment.

 ◦ Empowered to A.C.T.: ◦

What inspired **ACTION** will you take today?
What purposeful **CHANGE** will you make today?
What can you **TEACH** someone else today?

Happy Empowering Questions!

Remember, nothing happens until you decide to take action!

WHY Do You Listen?

"Great salespeople don't listen in order to anything. They simply listen. They listen because they are interested in the other person; they are curious. They want to know the person. They listen to learn."

~ Bob Burg

Not too long ago I was in a class where the instructor taught us how to pretend to be interested in someone else. I was flabbergasted! Pretend to be interested?! I couldn't believe this instructor actually thought to share this in the class! I mean, I see the value in teaching listening skills and such, but to teach how to be fake about it was over the top. It seemed manipulative to me. I invite you to throw away any and all pretending and to be a genuine and authentic listener! Be genuinely curious about people in general; ask quality questions and get to know them. People are fascinating creatures! You will find that out real quick if you take the time to be genuinely interested in people.

── Empowered to A.C.T.: ──

What inspired **ACTION** will you take today?
What purposeful **CHANGE** will you make today?
What can you **TEACH** someone else today?

Happy Being a Genuine Listener!

Remember, nothing happens until you decide to take action!

Think Outside Your Box!

"If we don't start thinking while we are in the box,
we'll never get out of the box to think."
~ Unknown

Did you know that almost 80% of our daily activities are habitual? That means the majority of people just go through the motions of their day on autopilot. It takes your conscious thinking, awareness, and desire to make new choices and not just do the same ole same ole every moment of every day. When you get out of autopilot mode and start thinking more consciously throughout your day, you see that you have more options, more opportunities, and therefore more choices! Stretch your mind and think outside the box!

⟶ Empowered to A.C.T.: ⟵

What inspired **ACTION** will you take today?
What purposeful **CHANGE** will you make today?
What can you **TEACH** someone else today?

Happy Thinking Bigger!

Remember, nothing happens until you decide to take action!

What Are Champions Made Of?

"Champions aren't made in gyms. Champions are made from something they have deep inside them a desire, a dream, a vision. They have to have the skill and the will. But the will must be stronger than the skill."
~ Muhammad Ali

I'm a huge advocate of specialized knowledge and am all for mastering skills; however, I believe so strongly all that doesn't matter unless you have a BURNING fire in your heart that fuels your will! You will give up long before you reach success or mastery if you don't have the deep burning desire, a dream, and a vision in your heart. Reignite that fire in your heart!

— Empowered to A.C.T.: —

What inspired **ACTION** will you take today?
What purposeful **CHANGE** will you make today?
What can you **TEACH** someone else today?

Happy Fire in Your Heart!

Remember, nothing happens until you decide to take action!

Shine a Light!

"Appreciation is the highest form of prayer, for it acknowledges the presence of good wherever you shine the light of your thankful thoughts."
~ Alan Cohen

What a beautiful quote! There is goodness all around us—all it takes is for us to feel it come alive in our hearts. It's our appreciation that highlights, underscores, and accentuates the beauty and gifts in something or someone. Look for more and more ways to express your appreciation and gratitude. Now, remember, you're not just looking for the "good" things to appreciate, but also challenge yourself to look beyond the surface and also appreciate the challenges and setbacks, for they too come bearing gifts that we can be grateful for.

Empowered to A.C.T.:

What inspired **ACTION** will you take today?
What purposeful **CHANGE** will you make today?
What can you **TEACH** someone else today?

Happy Shining a Light of Appreciation!

Remember, nothing happens until you decide to take action!

Ignite Love From Within Through Meditation

"If you meditate deeply, sooner or later you will start feeling tremendous love arising in you that you have never known before. You want a love which is born out of meditation, not born out of the mind."
~ Byron Embry

Ahhh, take a nice deep cleansing breath! Breathing deeply allows you to get out of your head and into your heart. Meditation is a great way to feel and experience love with ease. Find 15 or 20 minutes in your day today where you can be still and clear your mind. Breathe into your heart space and feel the love. Feel the love you have for all the amazing blessings in your life. Really allow yourself to FEEL and experience love from within. When you do, you will just naturally express it and share it with others. Focus on that feeling and allow it to bubble up and grow! Before you know it, you'll be oozing love!

Empowered to A.C.T.:

What inspired **ACTION** will you take today?
What purposeful **CHANGE** will you make today?
What can you **TEACH** someone else today?

Happy Oozing Love!

Remember, nothing happens until you decide to take action!

What Have You Been Planting?

"Always do your best. What you plant now, you will harvest later."
~ Og Mandino

The thoughts, feelings, and actions you plant now determine what you will harvest in your life. Think about it ... really think about what you are "planting." If you want to know what you have been planting up until this point, take a look at your current results. This harvest of current results you are getting in your life is a reflection of what thoughts, feelings, and actions you have been planting. If you see something you would like to change, begin to do your best at entertaining some new thoughts, ideas, and perspectives about your situation that serve you at a greater level. Alter your mindset and attitude because they are the determining factor in what you ultimately harvest.

⟋ Empowered to A.C.T.: ⟍

What inspired **ACTION** will you take today?
What purposeful **CHANGE** will you make today?
What can you **TEACH** someone else today?

Happy Planting New Thoughts, Feelings, and Actions!

Remember, nothing happens until you decide to take action!

Love is ALL there is!

"As you go along through the journeys of life,
you will discover that there is no substitute for love."
~ Francis K. Githinji

Love is ALL there is, my friend! I don't know about you, but I wouldn't even want there to be a substitute for love! I mean, it's not like a side dish at some restaurant or something. We are talking about true burning love for people, for animals, communities, nature … for everything!
Love is that emotion that makes your heart smile and shine brighter! It's the emotion that allows you to connect with someone at a deeper level. It's the emotion that allows you to be patient and forgiving. It's the emotion that calls forth a better version of yourself. It's the emotion that ignites you to want to give something your all! It's the emotion that knows at the end of the day, it's the most important emotion to embody!

Empowered to A.C.T.:

What inspired **ACTION** will you take today?
What purposeful **CHANGE** will you make today?
What can you **TEACH** someone else today?

Happy Embodying LOVE!

Remember, nothing happens until you decide to take action!

You Are Exactly Where You Need to Be!

"I seldom end up where I wanted to go, but almost always
end up where I need to be."
~ Douglas Adams

When you take a look at your life, there may be parts of it where you think to yourself, "How on earth did I end up here?!" I know I look at my life and think, "Wow, I never thought I'd be a Life and Business Success Coach living in North Carolina!" That wasn't on my radar 7 short years ago! The interesting thing though, is that I know I am exactly where I am supposed to be, doing exactly what I am supposed to be doing, and have never been more fulfilled in my life! That does not mean my life is always easy and everything works out perfectly. It just means that I have learned to trust life and know that whatever it presents to me and where ever it takes me, that it's exactly what I need in the moment. My days are packed with gifts, lessons, teachers, challenges, and adventures and they are all what I've needed to bring me to this day. Right here, right now. Now it's your turn. Take a look at where you are now in your life and reflect on how it's exactly where you need to be! Look at what you are learning, experiencing, and feeling. What lessons and gifts are here for you?

Empowered to A.C.T.:

What inspired **ACTION** will you take today?
What purposeful **CHANGE** will you make today?
What can you **TEACH** someone else today?

Happy Being Where You Need to Be!

Remember, nothing happens until you decide to take action!

What is Your Message to the World?

"Your life is your message to the world. Make it inspiring."
~ Lorrin L. Lee

Everything you say and do in your life projects a message. The great truth about this is that you get to choose what you say and do and therefore get to choose the message! Maybe the message you've been sending isn't the one you want to be sending. If that is the case, you can choose today to send a NEW, more inspiring message. Maybe it's one of hope and courage, strength and perseverance, or love and kindness. Think about what your message is in your career, to your family and friends, and to your community. Go WITHIN and discover your greater message, one that makes a great difference, a greater impact. Know that you are here for a special reason and that you were meant to leave an inspiring message for the world. People are meant to be inspired by you long after you are gone. What is your message to the world?

What inspired **ACTION** will you take today?
What purposeful **CHANGE** will you make today?
What can you **TEACH** someone else today?

Happy Inspiring Message!

Remember, nothing happens until you decide to take action!

See The Light!

"Faith is seeing light with your heart, when all your eyes see is the darkness ahead."
~ Unknown

When a situation appears to be dark, choose to see the light in the situation with your heart, not your eyes. On the physical level, you may never see the light in a dark and gloomy situation. You must go within. Go within your heart and reignite your faith. Reignite your belief in the unseen possibilities. Reignite your strength and courage to move forward. The beauty of faith is that it's ALWAYS there; it's just waiting on you to reignite it. And when you do, what emerges is so beautiful and bright, you will wonder why on earth you would go even another moment without living in faith. Walking in faith IS the way ... the only way!

⟿ Empowered to A.C.T.: ⟾

What inspired **ACTION** will you take today?
What purposeful **CHANGE** will you make today?
What can you **TEACH** someone else today?

Happy Reigniting and Living in Faith!

Remember, nothing happens until you decide to take action!

Today's Featured Reader:
Gail Ostrishko, Raleigh, North Carolina
"This is my favorite Daily W.O.W! I love the reminder that faith is always there, and we can reignite the light within; seeing the possibilities through your heart, not your eyes. I LOVE your W.O.W.'s and look forward to them daily. Thanks, Melissa."

Are You Making These Mistakes in Life?

"There are only two mistakes one can make along the road to truth; not going all the way, and not starting."

~ Buddha

The unfortunate thing is that most people struggle to get started and fulfill more of their true potential. And even if they do get started, many people only give enough to get by and settle for average. Here's the deal: there is no joy in not getting started and settling! The joy in life is in experiencing it! It's in giving it your all! The first gift to yourself is to get out of your own way and just get started. The second gift to yourself is to reach, stretch, and grow and see if you can crush your own records. You will learn more about who you really are, why you are here, and what you are really capable of by LIVING the life you were gifted!

Empowered to A.C.T.:

What inspired **ACTION** will you take today?
What purposeful **CHANGE** will you make today?
What can you **TEACH** someone else today?

Happy Getting Started and Going All the Way in Life!

Remember, nothing happens until you decide to take action!

You Irritated?

"If you are irritated by every rub, how will you be polished?"
~ Rumi

Life isn't meant to irritate you. Taking everything personally, looking to be offended, creating drama over everything, and being irritated by everyone, boy, oh, boy, what a toxic way to live. Not only is it toxic to your well-being, but it also prevents you from shining bright and enjoying life! It's hard to enjoy life and receive the many gifts it has to offer when you direct your energy toward that which drains you and drags you down. You'll shine your brightest when you aren't putting energy into taking things personally, looking for ways to be offended, creating drama, and being irritated. Your best self will rise to the surface and be expressed in a much healthier and productive manner. Everyone, including yourself, benefits from your light shining bright!

— Empowered to A.C.T.: —

What inspired **ACTION** will you take today?
What purposeful **CHANGE** will you make today?
What can you **TEACH** someone else today?

Happy Shining Bright!

Remember, nothing happens until you decide to take action!

Always Be a First-Rate You!

"Always be a first-rate version of yourself, instead of a second-rate version of somebody else."
~ Judy Garland

This quote is what I'm SOOOO passionate about! I believe so strongly in YOU BEING your BEST YOU and not in trying so hard to be somebody else! You may get caught up in what society and everyone else thinks is right for you, who you "should be," and with what everyone else is doing that you just end up growing further and further away from the REAL and AUTHENTIC YOU! When you allow and honor who you are on the inside to emerge and you live that to the fullest, your BEST YOU shines through and that's when your best work comes out! Nobody does a better job of you being you than you!

― Empowered to A.C.T.: ―

What inspired **ACTION** will you take today?
What purposeful **CHANGE** will you make today?
What can you **TEACH** someone else today?

Happy YOU Being YOU!

Remember, nothing happens until you decide to take action!

Savor the Present Moment

"Be present. Be here. Be now."
~ Unknown

I believe that the beauty and fulfillment of life resides within being present. When you are present, you get to experience so much more out of every waking moment! You FEEL more of your experiences! You don't just go through the motions of life, but rather you experience them in a way that creates real and powerful emotions within you. This is like when you scarf down a meal and you don't even remember what it tasted like versus eating a meal and savoring each bite and letting all the flavors come alive. YUM! It can feel like two totally different meals! Call yourself into the present moment as much as you can today and savor each moment and each experience! Feel the difference it makes in your day!

Empowered to A.C.T.:

What inspired **ACTION** will you take today?
What purposeful **CHANGE** will you make today?
What can you **TEACH** someone else today?

Happy Being Present and Savoring Life!

Remember, nothing happens until you decide to take action!

Cherish Your Vision!

"Cherish your visions and your dreams, as they are the children of your soul; the blueprints of your ultimate achievements."
~ Napoleon Hill

What is your vision and what are your dreams? Many people lack clarity when it comes to knowing what their vision and dreams are. If that's the case, it's important to put some time and energy into developing them. Take a few nice deep cleansing breaths and get into your heart space. Ask yourself, "What does my heart really have a burning desire for? What am I inspired to create in my life? What would it look like? And why is that important to me?" Really get clear on your answers. Your answers will help you develop a vision. Here is a little tip to know if you are on track with your vision or not: make sure your vision excites you, it energizes you, it ignites your passion, and you have a burning desire to make it your reality! When it does, it makes it easy to CHERISH it!

─ Empowered to A.C.T.: ─

What inspired **ACTION** will you take today?
What purposeful **CHANGE** will you make today?
What can you **TEACH** someone else today?

Happy Cherished Visions!

Remember, nothing happens until you decide to take action!

Today's Featured Reader:
Trent S. White, Thayne, Wyoming
"Thanks, Melissa, this has helped me see more clearly what I desire in my own journey."

Gratitude is Sooooo Good!

"Authentic gratitude is a way of life. When you wake up in the morning let your first thought be one of thanksgiving that you have another day to walk in the love of God. As you go through your day, see the GIVER behind all the gifts being given to you."
~ Michael Bernard Beckwith

I love how Michael Beckwith says gratitude is a "way of life." It's not something we just turn on and off when we feel like it, but rather it is a way of being. Make getting into a state of gratitude part of your daily rituals. When I feel grateful and express my gratitude, it always puts me in a state of joy and love. I can feel my energy shift into these states and I automatically feel myself starting to smile and have a warm heart. It's soooo good! How about you? Can you feel the shift? Let's try it right here and now ... take a moment right now to identify what you are truly and genuinely grateful for today. Know this, gratitude must be genuine and true in order for it to shift your energy and create miracles in your life!

Empowered to A.C.T.:

What inspired **ACTION** will you take today?
What purposeful **CHANGE** will you make today?
What can you **TEACH** someone else today?

Happy Gratitude!

Remember, nothing happens until you decide to take action!

How Have You Served Today?

"The best way to find yourself is to lose yourself in the service of others."
~ Mahatma Gandhi

When you are doing what you love and are meant to do, you can't help but get lost in it! I remember when I was teaching a coaching class for a fellow coach of mine up in Chicago for the day. I was having a blast and loving every second of it. As I left the class and headed back home, I realized I never charged the students the fee for attending the class! I had just done a 3 hour class for FREE! Actually, it cost ME because I had to drive 90 minutes there and 90 minutes back! As I headed home, I wanted to kick myself, but then I called a friend and she read this Gandhi quote to me. I thought it was absolutely perfect and it immediately changed my perception on what had just happened. How can you go the extra mile and over deliver your services today? I'm not saying to do them for free per se, but I'm encouraging you to see how you can get lost in the love of delivering them.

⟶ Empowered to A.C.T.: ⟵

What inspired **ACTION** will you take today?
What purposeful **CHANGE** will you make today?
What can you **TEACH** someone else today?

Happy Serving Others!

Remember, nothing happens until you decide to take action!

Does Your Thinking Limit You?

"Every man is free to rise as far as he is able or willing, but the degree to which he THINKS determines the degree to which he will rise."
~ Ayn Rand

If the degree to which someone will rise depends on their level of thinking, then what is one's level of thinking dependent upon? It's their level of SELF-AWARENESS! You see, you will never out-think your level of self-awareness. If you lack the self-awareness of who you really are and what you are really capable of, you will never think higher and greater of yourself and your possibilities. You will always limit yourself and get caught thinking less than and will settle in life. Raise your level of self-awareness to see who you really are in your heart and soul. See your true gifts, talents, value, and capabilities. As you do, your thinking will expand and you will find yourself rising above!

⸺ Empowered to A.C.T.: ⸺

What inspired **ACTION** will you take today?
What purposeful **CHANGE** will you make today?
What can you **TEACH** someone else today?

Happy Raising Your Level of Self-Awareness!

Remember, nothing happens until you decide to take action!

Do You Love It?

"I'd rather fail at something I love, than succeed at something I hate."
~ George Burns

I can relate to this quote because not early on when I started by career I was successful at working a job that wasn't really fulfilling me. I wouldn't say I "hated" it, but it definitely wasn't my true calling and didn't fill me up. It was really just a paycheck. Now that I'm following my true calling and living my dream as a coach, speaker, and trainer, I love every second of it, even the times I fall flat on my face! I gave a mini-presentation the other day that was pretty awful! It was like watching a train wreck take place and there was nothing I could do about it. Looking back, I still shake my head in embarrassment, but can laugh about it at the same time. Needless to say it wasn't my first, nor will it be my last train wreck presentation, but I'd rather endure a train wreck here and there if that means I get to live on purpose and continue doing what I LOVE! What about you? Do you do what you love?

Empowered to A.C.T.:

What inspired **ACTION** will you take today?
What purposeful **CHANGE** will you make today?
What can you **TEACH** someone else today?

Happy Doing What You Love!

Remember, nothing happens until you decide to take action!

You Gotta Love Change!

"When change happens, you can either cooperate with it and learn how to benefit from it or you can resist it and eventually get run over by it."
~ Jack Canfield

You gotta love change ... because change loves YOU! Change is great in the fact that it doesn't discriminate against anyone for any reason. Change is something that is happening all the time and is inevitable. With that said, it's important for you to find a place in your heart where you can embrace and welcome change knowing that the truth of life is change! Living life is all about you reaching, stretching, and growing and benefiting from the change that's taking place all around you! Without change you have nothing! Successful people look for ways to learn and benefit from whatever change is happening in their life. Go with the flow of change instead of trying to resist it.

─◦ Empowered to A.C.T.: ◦─

What inspired **ACTION** will you take today?
What purposeful **CHANGE** will you make today?
What can you **TEACH** someone else today?

Happy Happy Change!

Remember, nothing happens until you decide to take action!

Approve of Yourself!

"A man cannot be comfortable without his own approval."
~ Mark Twain

So often we are seeking outside approval in order to feel worthy, accepted, and happy with who we are. We may seek it from a parent, a spouse, a boss, a friend, etc. However, until you find it in your OWN heart to approve, accept, and love yourself, you will continue to seek and long for it as well as continue to be dependent upon others to feel that sense of worthiness and acceptance. The issue with someone else supplying you your worth, is that then they can take it away from you as fast as they can give it! Find it in your OWN heart to approve, accept, and love yourself. You will find your greatest fulfillment there!

— Empowered to A.C.T.: —

What inspired **ACTION** will you take today?
What purposeful **CHANGE** will you make today?
What can you **TEACH** someone else today?

Happy Self-Approval!

Remember, nothing happens until you decide to take action!

March

Are You Courageous?

"Life shrinks or expands in proportion to one's courage."
~ Anais Nin

We all have an unlimited amount of courage within us! Yes, unlimited! It is not that someone has courage and someone else doesn't have any courage, but rather there are times when a person does not call it forth and exercise it. They may convince themselves they "do not have the courage or strength" to do something. That's absolutely false! If you agree that you have unlimited courage within you, then it begs the question of, how do I call forth and exercise more of my courage?

Well, you must exercise the part of you that sees and believes in your greater and stronger self. You could say empowering affirmations and prayers. You could journal, visualize, or meditate. Start today by exercising your courage and watch the life you create expand to a whole new dimension!

─◦ Empowered to A.C.T.: ◦─

What inspired **ACTION** will you take today?
What purposeful **CHANGE** will you make today?
What can you **TEACH** someone else today?

Happy Courage!

Remember, nothing happens until you decide to take action!

Accept Responsibility

"There two primary choices in life: to accept conditions as they exist, or accept the responsibility for changing them."
~ Denis Waitley

Nobody is going to go out there and create the perfect life FOR YOU. You either accept the cards you have been dealt or you ask for a new hand. I say, if you are unhappy then ask for a new hand! Here you can design and create a life you truly desire for yourself and your family with great intention and purpose. There's no need to complain about current conditions and circumstances in your life ... just accept the responsibility for changing them and get to work! You know you have the power to change your current situation ... you know that, right?! What you need to do to achieve a new outcome?

⁓ Empowered to A.C.T.: ⁓

What inspired **ACTION** will you take today?
What purposeful **CHANGE** will you make today?
What can you **TEACH** someone else today?

Happy Accepting Responsibility For Your Life!

Remember, nothing happens until you decide to take action!

What Are You On?

"Every man is enthusiastic at times. One man has enthusiasm for thirty minutes, another man has it for thirty days. But it is the man who has it for thirty years who makes a success in life."
~ Edward B. Butler

How do you know when you are an enthusiastic person? You know when you are often asked, "You have so much energy and enthusiasm, what are you on?" That's when you are right on track! I pretty much ooze enthusiasm and get asked on a regular basis, "What am I on?" and it just reminds me how happy I am and how much I am enjoying this wonderful life of mine. I am not saying my life is perfect by any means. I go through the same ups and downs as everyone else. I just choose to be happy and enthusiastic rather than down in the dumps. Wouldn't you agree that you too feel more amazing and more alive when you ooze enthusiasm? Actually, enthusiasm and depression are just one thought away from each other. Which one do you choose today?

What inspired **ACTION** will you take today?
What purposeful **CHANGE** will you make today?
What can you **TEACH** someone else today?

Happy Choosing Enthusiasm!

Remember, nothing happens until you decide to take action!

What Does Authenticity Mean?

"Authenticity doesn't mean you can't use preplanned words. It just means that when you do, you have to make them your own, in both your head and your heart."
~ Bob Burg

I love this! I am all for practice, practice, practice. I love to polish up a keynote, a workshop, an elevator pitch, etc. However, a MUST to all of my communications both professional and personal is that they are ME and they come from my heart. I am terrible at using someone else's scripted words that don't resonate with me. I feel awkward and fake when I try and force myself to say something inauthentic. I don't have the same confidence and poise I have with my own words. How about you? Do you feel that way too? Be true to yourself! Be authentic!

— Empowered to A.C.T.: —

What inspired **ACTION** will you take today?
What purposeful **CHANGE** will you make today?
What can you **TEACH** someone else today?

Happy Being Authentically You!

Remember, nothing happens until you decide to take action!

Shhhhhh!

"Calmness of mind is one of the beautiful jewels of wisdom."
~ James Allen

Shhhhhhh! Can you hear that? Silence! Ahhhhhh! Isn't it music to your mind, body, and soul when you cause an interruption in the mind chatter?! That mind chatter can drain you and consume your every ounce of energy! When your mind is running wild, you miss out on the gift this present moment comes bearing. You miss out on the inner message and guidance that you are meant to receive in the here and now. Shhhhhhh! Calm your mind. Ask for guidance, yet be still enough to allow the answer to come into your awareness. When your mind is running wild, there is no room for the answer to enter! Create a space for it ... calm and clear your monkey mind. Welcome the answers!

~ Empowered to A.C.T.: ~

What inspired **ACTION** will you take today?
What purposeful **CHANGE** will you make today?
What can you **TEACH** someone else today?

Happy Shhhhhhh!

Remember, nothing happens until you decide to take action!

Believe in the Unseen!

"Life has its seasons … and regardless of the season,
the sun always shines!"
~ Melissa West (Malueg)

Over the last few weeks, the weather has been a wet and gray here in North
Carolina. I've noticed the sun has been hiding behind the clouds a lot more
than usual. I love the sunshine, so I definitely notice when the skies are gray and
cloudy. I remind myself that just because the sky is full of clouds, doesn't mean
the sun isn't shining brighter than ever behind them. It reminds me to have faith
and believe in the unseen even when things aren't always going as planned. Just
because you can't see everything with your physical sight, doesn't mean something
amazing isn't happening there. Remind yourself of this as you work toward
creating your goals. You may not always see all the pieces coming together. Fuel
your faith and desire and know it's working. Just keep forging ahead with your
focus, intention, and burning desire!

⌐ Empowered to A.C.T.: ⌐

What inspired **ACTION** will you take today?
What purposeful **CHANGE** will you make today?
What can you **TEACH** someone else today?

Happy Believing in the Unseen!

Remember, nothing happens until you decide to take action!

Rejoice in Your Blessings!

"He is a wise man who does not grieve for the things which he has not, but rejoices for those which he has."

~ Epictetus

Take a moment to rejoice in all that you ARE, all that you have achieved, and all that you have! See how blessed you really are. I invite you to really really focus on all that YOU ARE! Notice YOUR unique gifts, talents, and purpose in life. Really see how you have made a difference in this world, whether it was one life or a thousand lives, really see how it was YOU that made that difference. Rejoice and be grateful! You see, it's what's in your heart and soul that we should rejoice in. That's your true essence and all the other creations we celebrate come from you expressing and sharing yourself with the world. All the wonderful people, things, and experiences in your life are just a reflection of who you are in the inside.

Rejoice and be grateful!

Empowered to A.C.T.:

What inspired **ACTION** will you take today?
What purposeful **CHANGE** will you make today?
What can you **TEACH** someone else today?

Happy YOU!

Remember, nothing happens until you decide to take action!

You Can Turn a Life Around!

"Too often we underestimate the power of a touch, a smile, a kind word, a listening ear, an honest compliment, or the smallest act of caring, all of which have the potential to turn a life around."
~ Leo Buscaglia

Don't underestimate the great value that comes in small packages! This quote reminded me that it's the little things that go a long way and make a huge difference. Often we think we don't have the time, energy, or money to make a difference. However, when we take a step back and look at what DOES make a difference and matters most, it's all those special moments when someone expresses their care and love for us. Do you notice a difference in yourself when you are surrounded by smiling, laughing, loving, and kind people? They DO have an impact on you, don't they? They add light to our days! Well, you do the same for others ... so spread the love and light, my friends! It all starts with YOU!

—◦ Empowered to A.C.T.: ◦—

What inspired **ACTION** will you take today?
What purposeful **CHANGE** will you make today?
What can you **TEACH** someone else today?

Happy Making a Difference!

Remember, nothing happens until you decide to take action!

Never Ending Wealth!

"I can keep on giving because there is no end to my wealth. I am pleased to offer my surplus to others."
~ Wayne Dyer

Do you think like this ... in abundance? Or do you think the opposite ... in lack? Many people get caught up in the lack mentality. Let's face it, though, we live in a society that focuses more on the lack than the abundance! It can be easy to get caught up and stuck in a mindset that thinks there is a limited supply of wealth available to all of us. That is completely false, false, false! Not true, my friends! It is up to each and every one of you to make sure you are feeding your mind and soul thoughts and experiences of abundance, prosperity, and never ending joy and love! There is NO limit! My advice to you is to BE an open channel to RECEIVING wealth so you have more to GIVE!

—◦ Empowered to A.C.T.: ◦—

What inspired **ACTION** will you take today?
What purposeful **CHANGE** will you make today?
What can you **TEACH** someone else today?

Happy Never Ending Wealth!

Remember, nothing happens until you decide to take action!

Are You Listening?

"If you are not going to listen, then don't ask anymore."
~ God

How often do you pray for the clarity, insight and solutions to a difficult or confusing situation, but then neglect to be open to receiving the answers? So often we are being internally guided by our gut, our intuition, our heart, our spirit, God, and it is trying to get our attention and guide us. Unfortunately, too often, we ignore and don't listen to that inner guidance. Next time you pray, include in your prayers the energy to stay open and listen for answers and solutions; to receive them, to trust them, and to follow through on them, knowing that they came from a higher part of you.

⁓ Empowered to A.C.T.: ⁓

What inspired **ACTION** will you take today?
What purposeful **CHANGE** will you make today?
What can you **TEACH** someone else today?

Happy Listening!

Remember, nothing happens until you decide to take action!

Crush Your Own Records!

"A creative man is motivated by the desire to achieve,
not by the desire to beat others."
~ Ayn Rand

Some think that the point of being competitive is so you can celebrate in the victory of crushing your opponent. Well, I actually believe there is a much healthier and more exhilarating way to compete and that is to compete with yourself. Seek to crush YOUR OWN records, play YOUR best game, and show up YOUR best self! Constantly focusing on the other person as a benchmark of your growth and success is just blocking your own creativity. Instead, use their experiences as part of your research and data collecting on how you can alter your approach. Then focus on how you can reach, stretch, grow, outdo yourself, and go where you have never gone before!

—◦ Empowered to A.C.T.: ◦—

What inspired **ACTION** will you take today?
What purposeful **CHANGE** will you make today?
What can you **TEACH** someone else today?

Happy Crushing Your Own Records!

Remember, nothing happens until you decide to take action!

Encourage and Support Change, Don't Force It!

"Before you try and change others,
remember how hard it is to change yourself."
~ Bill Bluestein

I find it funny how we can be so adamant with changing others, but when it comes to ourselves, we resist change. My sister and I laugh because we love giving each other advice and trying to help each other make changes; however, most of the time we both resist the advice and end up doing whatever we want to do anyways. We used to get offended when the other one wouldn't take our advice, but now we have a greater understanding of change and how you really can't make someone change. You can encourage, support, and be there for them, but at the end of the day, it's up to them to change themselves. We are much better at being encouragers and supporters than we are at forcing change, especially for other people. Be an encourager and a supporter today!

—◦ Empowered to A.C.T.: ◦—

What inspired **ACTION** will you take today?
What purposeful **CHANGE** will you make today?
What can you **TEACH** someone else today?

Happy Supporting and Encouraging Change!

Remember, nothing happens until you decide to take action!

Are You Reluctant to do the Inner Work?

"Most people are anxious to improve their circumstances but unwilling to improve themselves. They are either reluctant to do the inner work of self-reflection or simply don't know how. However, consider this; it is easier to change yourself than it is to change others. When you realize this simple truth, you will begin to understand the importance of uncovering and understanding your authentic self."
~ Lou Cassara

I love this quote! It speaks right to my heart! Probably because helping others grow from the inside out is my purpose in life! I am so passionate about wanting others to see the value in their authentic selves. Unfortunately, many people are reluctant to do the inner work. I am here to share with you that the inner work is the KEY to your success! It's the foundation to all personal growth. You can't maintain your success without growing from the inside out. The same person who achieved the goal isn't the same person it will take to maintain it and go beyond it. Go into today open and willing to do the inner work!

— Empowered to A.C.T.: —

What inspired **ACTION** will you take today?
What purposeful **CHANGE** will you make today?
What can you **TEACH** someone else today?

Happy Inner Growth!

Remember, nothing happens until you decide to take action!

Courage Comes Through Taking Risks

"Courage can only come through experiences where we run a risk, take a chance—
we win some and we lose some."
~ Robert H. Schuller

If you never take any risks, you'll never get to experience your own courage. It doesn't take much courage at all to stay in your comfort zone and not seek to reach, stretch, and grow. Besides, life gets too boring when you never take a chance and grow! Today I invite you to step out of your comfort zone and experience your courage! Do something that you've been putting off and making excuses for. The outcome may be in your favor… or it may not be. The point is that you don't know the outcome for sure and therefore you must ignite the courage within to support you along the way so you stay committed and focused on your goal!

⸻ Empowered to A.C.T.: ⸻

What inspired **ACTION** will you take today?
What purposeful **CHANGE** will you make today?
What can you **TEACH** someone else today?

Happy Experiencing Your Courage!

Remember, nothing happens until you decide to take action!

Are You Dedicated to Your Growth?

"Facing difficulties is inevitable. Learning from them is optional. Whether you learn is based on if you understand that difficulties present opportunities to learn and treat them accordingly."
~ John C. Maxwell

Whatever difficulty you are experiencing right now is exactly what you are meant to be going through and learning from. There is a lesson, an opportunity, something to be gained from the experience … if you choose to see it that way. So often we miss out on the opportunity to learn and grow from our pain because we aren't looking for it. But if you take a moment and really contemplate on the experience before you, you'll see that you are meant to come out a stronger, more evolved human being. Be dedicated to your growth and to always finding the lesson, the opportunity within your pain. Oh, yes, it's in there, so don't give up! Be dedicated to your growth!

—◦ Empowered to A.C.T.: ◦—

What inspired **ACTION** will you take today?
What purposeful **CHANGE** will you make today?
What can you **TEACH** someone else today?

Happy Being Dedicated to Your Growth!

Remember, nothing happens until you decide to take action!

No Need to Conform

"Conformity is the jailer of freedom and the enemy of growth."
~ John F. Kennedy

Were you taught to conform? Were you taught to look, do, and say what everyone is looking like, doing, and saying? I think most of us were taught to live that way in one form or another and to varying degrees. I don't know about you, but I know when I get caught up in trying to look like everyone else, do what everyone else is doing, and say what everyone else is saying, I DON'T feel like myself and I feel like I'm trying to be someone I'm not. I find myself self-judging my every move. On the contrary, when I look to others as my teachers, mentors, and guides, I know they are in my life to help guide me to reach, stretch, and grow into being my BEST ME! Choose to see others as guides, not as someone you need to conform to and become an exact replica of.

— Empowered to A.C.T.: —

What inspired **ACTION** will you take today?
What purposeful **CHANGE** will you make today?
What can you **TEACH** someone else today?

Happy Reaching, Stretching, and Growing into Your Uniquely BEST Self!

Remember, nothing happens until you decide to take action!

The Opportunity is Right Here!

"Don't look for an opportunity.
The one you have in hand is the opportunity."
~ Paul Arden

So often we hope and pray and seek and search for the perfect opportunity. Sometimes it can feel like it's so far away and you may wonder and doubt if it will ever happen. What if you didn't need to look so far? What if your opportunity is right here and right now? You see, there isn't a lack of opportunities, there is just a lack of awareness of opportunities. Be aware that there is opportunity in every moment. If you seize that moment, it will lead you to your next opportunity to be seized! What opportunity is before you today? How will you seize it? Your opportunities are endless!

― Empowered to A.C.T.: ―

What inspired **ACTION** will you take today?
What purposeful **CHANGE** will you make today?
What can you **TEACH** someone else today?

Happy Opportunities Right Here, Right Now!

Remember, nothing happens until you decide to take action!

What Do You See?

"Life is just a mirror, and what you see out there,
you must first see inside yourself."
~ Jacob Bigelow

Take a good look at the world … what amazing and great things do you desire to create for yourself? Maybe it's an ideal relationship, a beautiful home, a meaningful career, a healthy family, to travel the world … whatever it may be, you must first begin to the close the gap on the idea that you are separate from those things. You must see them within you. You must see that you hold all the potential and resources necessary to create them WITHIN YOU. Do you see all the determination, focus, persistence, patience, and courage within you to create what you want to be, do, and have in your life? It's all there … call them forth!

─◦ Empowered to A.C.T.: ◦─

What inspired **ACTION** will you take today?
What purposeful **CHANGE** will you make today?
What can you **TEACH** someone else today?

Happy Calling Forth the Potential Within You!

Remember, nothing happens until you decide to take action!

Do You Resist Abundance?

"There is only allowing or resisting, allowing or denying,
letting in or keeping out the abundance that you deserve. When
your resistance stops, your abundance will come."
~ Esther Hicks (Teachings of Abraham)

You cannot think and feel abundant and lack at the same time. It's one or the other.
At times it may feel like you're thinking and feeling both, but you're really not.
You're just switching back and forth between the two. So, you cannot "sort of" allow
abundance into your life. You either allow it or you don't. As quickly as you can flip
a light switch on, you can change your thoughts and feelings toward yourself and
abundance. You can start by imagining amazing things happening all around you all
day long. Begin to see the abundance of beauty, life, and opportunity all around you!
There is no shortage, but you must change your thoughts and perception in order to
see it. Start there and before you know it, you'll be overwhelmed by the abundance of
beauty, life, and opportunity all around you!

Empowered to A.C.T.:

What inspired **ACTION** will you take today?
What purposeful **CHANGE** will you make today?
What can you **TEACH** someone else today?

Happy Abundance All Around You!

Remember, nothing happens until you decide to take action!

What Will They Remember About You?

"Live so that when your children think of fairness
and integrity, they think of you."
~ Unknown

My business partner, John C. Maxwell, often talks about how important it is to him to leave a legacy behind for his children and his children's children. That won't happen by accident. He chooses to make decisions that are always in alignment with that core value and belief of his. I admire him for doing so and it reminds me to do the same myself. I always seek to do my best and serve the best I can. It doesn't mean I'm perfect by any means, but I hope when people see me and think of me, they can sense my authentic desire to want to succeed and serve the best I can. What about you? What will you be remembered for? Are you deliberately working on your legacy?

Empowered to A.C.T.:

What inspired **ACTION** will you take today?
What purposeful **CHANGE** will you make today?
What can you **TEACH** someone else today?

Happy Creating a Legacy Worth Remembering!

Remember, nothing happens until you decide to take action!

Start Now!

"Nobody can go back and start a new beginning, but anyone can start today and make a new ending."
~ Maria Robinson

There is no need to beat yourself up with where you are at or the results you have gotten. Start anew! There is no need to focus on the past and get yourself frustrated with yesterday's happenings. Start anew! There is also no need to wait until you have hit rock bottom before you choose to transform your life. Start anew! Start shifting your thought process to a more positive and uplifting one! Embrace the lessons learned and start on a new path. Choose to fill your mind with thoughts that encourage you to keep putting one foot in front of the other. Incorporate a daily practice of reading or meditation where you fill yourself up in a positive way, EVERY DAY! What I like to do every day is read and/or listen to an uplifting CD, meditate, and journal every evening before I go to bed. It may seem like a lot to do, but believe me, my mind, heart and soul thanks me for it every day and night.

⚬ Empowered to A.C.T.: ⚬

What inspired **ACTION** will you take today?
What purposeful **CHANGE** will you make today?
What can you **TEACH** someone else today?

Happy Happy Starting Anew!

Remember, nothing happens until you decide to take action!

You are a Divine Spirit!

"People go through challenging moments of losing people and of having their
life threatened from illness and real grief, but they all get through it.
This is a testament to the human spirit and it is where we are fragile,
but we are also divine."
~ Sheryl Crow

There are moments when every ounce of our spirit is being tested. We have to
dig deep and find within us the strength and courage to make it through some of
life's greatest trials and tribulations. These can be some of the most challenging
moments in our lives. However, during these challenging moments we get to
experience our truth, our divinity, the infinite power that is flowing to, with, and
through us. It's an amazing experience to see light come from what appears to be
darkness! You are a divine spirit, my friend!

—◦ Empowered to A.C.T.: ◦—

What inspired **ACTION** will you take today?
What purposeful **CHANGE** will you make today?
What can you **TEACH** someone else today?

Happy Divine Spirits!

Remember, nothing happens until you decide to take action!

Be a Go-Giver

"A pessimist, they say, sees a glass of water as being half-empty; an optimist sees the same glass as half-full. But a giving person sees a glass of water and starts looking for someone who might be thirsty."
~ G. Donald Gale

This quote is so beautiful and reminds me of one of my all-time favorite books, *The Go-Giver* by Bob Burg and John David Mann. It's such an amazing book jam-packed with a lot of heart and a lot of power. The book perfectly illustrates how when you look beyond yourself and be of service to others and help others create what they desire, that you will receive more than you ever imagined. It's the Law of Giving and Receiving! The important idea here, though, is that you don't go looking to be of service solely to "get" something in return, but rather you give and be of service for the sake of being of service because you enjoy it!

Empowered to A.C.T.:

What inspired **ACTION** will you take today?
What purposeful **CHANGE** will you make today?
What can you **TEACH** someone else today?

Happy Being a Go-Giver!

Remember, nothing happens until you decide to take action!

Confidence Comes from the Inside Out

"Being naturally confident isn't about how you act on the outside, it's about how you feel within which exudes on the outside."
~ Carla Cunningham

A phony can be spotted a mile away! Don't try and fake your confidence, but rather truly embody it and become it. Think about what it would really feel like to be genuinely and naturally confident. Think about it. Your shoulders would be relaxed, your breathing would be deep and controlled, your face would be relaxed and warm, your natural personality would flow right out of you, your words would be spoken with conviction, and above all, your heart would be smiling proud! That, my friends, you cannot fake! Claim it, own it, be it—from the inside out!

Empowered to A.C.T.:

What inspired **ACTION** will you take today?
What purposeful **CHANGE** will you make today?
What can you **TEACH** someone else today?

Happy Natural Confidence!

Remember, nothing happens until you decide to take action!

Do You Feel Inferior?

"Remember, no one can make you feel inferior without your consent."
~ Eleanor Roosevelt

Are you aware of your greatness? For real now … do you know how magnificent and powerful you really are? It's kind of sad how easily we hand over our greatness and power every now and then when someone "makes" us feel inferior and less than. We step out of our greatness and into a shadow of darkness. Those types of experiences are easy to blame others for and then we say they are controlling, mean, and overbearing. I invite you to pause here for a moment and take a greater look at what's going on. We blame others for "making" us feel bad and less than; however, that is not possible unless WE are allowing it. No one, absolutely no one, can take your greatness and power unless you hand it over. Choose to stand tall and confident in your magnificence and power!

— Empowered to A.C.T.: —

What inspired **ACTION** will you take today?
What purposeful **CHANGE** will you make today?
What can you **TEACH** someone else today?

Happy Standing in Your Greatness and Power!

Remember, nothing happens until you decide to take action!

Have You Started Yet?

"Don't wait until everything is just right. It will never be perfect. There will always be challenges, obstacles and less than perfect conditions. So what. Get started now. With each step you take, you will grow stronger and stronger, more and more skilled, more and more self-confident and more and more successful."
~ Mark Victor Hansen

Do you ever wait to leave your house in the morning until all of the street lights have turned green? I didn't think so … because if you did, you would NEVER leave your house! So why wait for all things to be perfect in other areas of your life before getting started and moving forward? You may be waiting for the day when all your fear is gone, you have a 100% rock solid belief in yourself, and you have a surge of passion and energy ready to take on any challenge that comes you way. Well, that day may never come, so stop waiting for it and get to work with where you are at! There will never be a perfect time to get started with something new and/or to keep at what you're working on. START TODAY! Your BEST LIFE is waiting for YOU!

⟶ Empowered to A.C.T.: ⟵

What inspired **ACTION** will you take today?
What purposeful **CHANGE** will you make today?
What can you **TEACH** someone else today?

Happy GETTING STARTED!

Remember, nothing happens until you decide to take action!

The Law of Attraction in Action!

"You cannot attract the presence of something wanted
when you are predominately aware of its absence."
~ Esther Hicks (Teachings of Abraham)

Think of one thing that your heart desires. It may be something regarding your career, it may be a material item, it may be a soulmate. Regardless of what it is, I want you to think about it for a moment. Are you thinking about it yet? OK, now I want you to observe your thoughts regarding that goal and desire. Do your thoughts remind you that you don't have it yet, that it's not in your life yet, and that you long for it to be? If so, you are just affirming its absence and guess what? You are attracting more absence, longing, and wanting ... instead of HAVING it already. Think about your goals and desires in a way that they are already in your life. They are here and you are enjoying them. GIVE THANKS for them! This way you will be affirming you have already created it and are attracting it into your life.

⟶ Empowered to A.C.T.: ⟵

What inspired **ACTION** will you take today?
What purposeful **CHANGE** will you make today?
What can you **TEACH** someone else today?

Happy Law of Attraction in action!

Remember, nothing happens until you decide to take action!

Pain is an Eye Opener

"Each time we encounter a painful experience, we get to know ourselves a little better. Pain can stop us dead in our tracks. Or it can cause us to make decisions we would like to put off, deal with issues we would rather not face, and make changes that make us feel uncomfortable. Pain prompts us to face who we are and where we are."
~ John C. Maxwell

Pain isn't the "happiest" topic; however, believe it or not, pain comes with great gifts too! Pain is an eye opener! It can be like looking in a mirror and seeing yourself more clearly, who you are being, where you are at, and what needs your attention. If you acknowledge the pain you're having as a clue or a message of some kind, you will receive something totally different from the experience than if you just muscled your way through it and suppressed the pain without ever addressing the real issue at hand. I encourage you today to face your pain. There's a great opportunity to learn something new that will change your life forever!

⌒ Empowered to A.C.T.: ⌒

What inspired **ACTION** will you take today?
What purposeful **CHANGE** will you make today?
What can you **TEACH** someone else today?

Happy Facing Your Pain!

Remember, nothing happens until you decide to take action!

See the Potential in Every Moment

"Don't wait for the perfect moment. Take the moment and make it perfect!"
~ Unknown

Believe it or not, you have much more control over your every moment than you think! Every moment has the potential to be perfect. However, it's up to YOU to see the potential in every moment. Allow yourself to look beyond the blocks and barriers and see the opportunity in this very moment, right here, right now; big or small. If all you see are blocks and barriers then you will be much more inclined to sit back and be passed up by the person next to you who is seizing the moment!

⁘ Empowered to A.C.T.: ⁘

What inspired **ACTION** will you take today?
What purposeful **CHANGE** will you make today?
What can you **TEACH** someone else today?

Happy Seizing the Moment!

Remember, nothing happens until you decide to take action!

The Law of Intentionality

"The Law of Intentionality: Growth doesn't just happen. You
have to grow with intention and purpose."
~ John C. Maxwell

Growth doesn't happen by accident! It doesn't just fall in your lap. At times I
wish it did, but that's not how your growth and development works. It requires
you being deliberate and intentional about what it is that you choose to create and
experience in your life. Live your life by DESIGN, not by DEFAULT! What is it
that you intend to create and experience in your life in the next 6 months? What is
the greater purpose for these creations and experiences? What is your growth plan
to move forward in the direction this vision? Intend to wake up every morning and
take purposeful action toward your answers to these questions!

─◦ Empowered to A.C.T.: ◦─

What inspired **ACTION** will you take today?
What purposeful **CHANGE** will you make today?
What can you **TEACH** someone else today?

Happy Being Intentional!

Remember, nothing happens until you decide to take action!

Find The Good That Surrounds You

"Many people fail to recognize the good things that happen in their
lives every day that the sun rises."
~ Paulo Coelho

When we have a lot going on in life, especially when we have a lot of drama and
conflict, it can be easy to look past the good things happening in life. Never let
the drama of outside circumstances and people disconnect you from the gratitude
in your heart. Find a way to express gratitude for even the simplest things in life
… for what if the simple things were some of the most important things? The sun
rising, your heart beating, the air in your lungs, the food on your table, the eyes
that are reading this message. Give thanks, my friends!

Empowered to A.C.T.:

What inspired **ACTION** will you take today?
What purposeful **CHANGE** will you make today?
What can you **TEACH** someone else today?

Happy Recognizing the Good that Surrounds You!

Remember, nothing happens until you decide to take action!

Today's Featured Reader:
Heidi Endicott, Milwaukee, Wisconsin
"I love all of your posts on Gratitude, but this one really puts in perspective to remind me
of looking all around you for gratitude. Like in the book 8 to Great, writing down one
thing to be grateful for everyday really makes you start to watch and put gratitude into a
whole other level. Thank you, Melissa!"

April

Build Enjoyable Relationships

"Communication is critical to developing mutually beneficial and mutually enjoyable relationships. Relationships require trust, and one of the best ways to develop trust is to focus on helping the other person feel heard and understood."
~ Jack Canfield

When it comes to building enjoyable relationships, trust is at the core. If you don't trust someone, the relationship will be far from enjoyable! Remember, we befriend and do business with those we know, like and trust. With that said how can you build upon your relationships and develop an even stronger trust? A basic need that everyone has is to be heard and understood. People feel a great deal of connection and significance when they feel heard and understood. Make it a goal of yours today to actively listen, ask open-ended questions, and validate what your friends, loved ones, and colleagues have to say and then watch how much more enjoyable those relationships become!

⟿ Empowered to A.C.T.: ⟿

What inspired **ACTION** will you take today?
What purposeful **CHANGE** will you make today?
What can you **TEACH** someone else today?

Happy Enjoyable Relationships!

Remember, nothing happens until you decide to take action!

What is a Problem?

"Problems are not stops signs, they are guidelines."
~ Robert H. Schuller

What are your problems and your fears trying to tell you? I can tell you what they are NOT saying … they are NOT saying STOP, they are NOT saying GIVE UP, and I know for sure they are NOT saying YOU CAN'T HANDLE IT! What if your problems and your fears were trying to tell you to KEEP GOING and YOU CAN DO IT, but you just need to make a few adjustments? What if your problems are just feedback? What if your fear is just trying to get your attention so that something could be tweaked and adjusted in your life that would serve you in a great way? Take a look at a problem or a fear you might be dealing with right now. What is it really trying to tell you? What's the real message? What could you do differently to get new results?

— Empowered to A.C.T.: —

What inspired **ACTION** will you take today?
What purposeful **CHANGE** will you make today?
What can you **TEACH** someone else today?

Happy Feedback!

Remember, nothing happens until you decide to take action!

What Will Be Your Legacy?

"The Law of Legacy: What do you want people to say at your funeral? That may seem like an odd question, but it may be the most important thing you can ask yourself as a leader. Why? Because a leader's lasting value is measured by succession."
~ John C. Maxwell

The direction you are heading in is hopefully putting you in a position to leave something positive behind for others. Think about what it is that you want others to carry on in your memory and continue to share with the generations to come. More than you know, you are making an impact on many lives. The choice is yours as to whether that impact will be positive or negative. Start thinking now about where you are spending your time and how you are creating your legacy. What do you want to be remembered for and WHY? Why is it important to you to be remembered for that? Really connect and fall in love with your legacy!

Empowered to A.C.T.:

What inspired **ACTION** will you take today?
What purposeful **CHANGE** will you make today?
What can you **TEACH** someone else today?

Happy Lasting Legacy!

Remember, nothing happens until you decide to take action!

Are You a Pessimist or Optimist?

"A stumbling block to the pessimist is a stepping stone to the optimist."
~ Eleanor Roosevelt

As you begin your day, are you going into the day as a pessimist or an optimist? Do you see the day ahead as full of roadblocks or full of opportunities to go down a new path and grow forward? Do you back away from them or step toward them? It's all in your perception of the path before you: stumbling blocks or stepping stones? Sometimes it can be challenging to alter your perception and see the good and the opportunity in whatever the situation is before you. The key is to practice doing this all the time, no matter how big or small the challenge is! Be an optimist and find the opportunity! The more you do, the more natural it will be for you to always look for the good, the opportunity, the stepping stone and ultimately find the solution! Remember, nothing happens until you decide to take action! Leave a comment below about how you keep an optimistic attitude.

Empowered to A.C.T.:

What inspired **ACTION** will you take today?
What purposeful **CHANGE** will you make today?
What can you **TEACH** someone else today?

Happy Optimism Today and Every Day!

Remember, nothing happens until you decide to take action!

You Always Have a Choice!

"Choice is your greatest power. It is an even greater power than love, because you must first choose to be a loving person."
~ Caroline Myss

You always have a choice, even when it seems like you don't, you do. Always remember in every moment of your day, you have a choice of how you want to show up. Do you show up your best or your worst? Loving or irritated? Open or closed? Empowered or as a victim? YOU, and only you, decide the person you're going to be. No one can take that away from you. What an empowering feeling, right?! I believe your power of choice is such a gift because it enables you to create the days of your life through your choices. Your decisions determine your direction. Take responsibility for your ability to choose and make decisions. It's never too late to make a new choice and show up as a better version of yourself.

⌐◦ Empowered to A.C.T.: ◦⌐

What inspired **ACTION** will you take today?
What purposeful **CHANGE** will you make today?
What can you **TEACH** someone else today?

Happy Making Better Choices!

Remember, nothing happens until you decide to take action!

Cheers to New Beginnings!

"What appears to be the end may really be a new beginning."
~ Unknown

When something is ending it can literally feel like a death! It can be very hard to accept and move on. Some grieving and mourning may need to take place in order for you to heal, and that's totally normal. It is important that we express and release those emotions and not suppress them. Once you allow yourself that, you will feel excited and ready to welcome the new beginning ... the new life! With every death comes the birth of a new life! Where are you in the process of welcoming new beginnings? Have you given yourself permission to heal from past situations that may have hurt you or losses with unresolved anger or pain? If not, give yourself this gift so that you can move forward and welcome the new beginning that is waiting for you!

— Empowered to A.C.T.: —

What inspired **ACTION** will you take today?
What purposeful **CHANGE** will you make today?
What can you **TEACH** someone else today?

Happy New Beginnings!

Remember, nothing happens until you decide to take action!

What Are You Doing?

"Efficiency is doing things right. Effectiveness is doing the right things."
~ Peter Drucker

Where are you spending your time and energy? On doing THINGS RIGHT or on doing THE RIGHT THINGS? We can spend a lot of time and energy on tasks that aren't purposeful or serving us and our goals and that are not going to get us very far! Don't get caught up in spending time organizing your paperclips and pens (LOL!), but rather focus on the tasks that are of high priority and a purposeful part of your journey. I encourage you to stop and observe your activities today. Ask yourself if where you are spending your time and energy is purposeful and an expression of what you are seeking to create in your life.

⌐ Empowered to A.C.T.: ⌐

What inspired **ACTION** will you take today?
What purposeful **CHANGE** will you make today?
What can you **TEACH** someone else today?

Happy Doing the Right Things!

Remember, nothing happens until you decide to take action!

Got Good Karma? You Choose!

"How people treat you is their karma; how you react is yours."
~ Wayne Dyer

Think of your reactions to all people and experiences as a glimpse into your future. How you choose to respond to people and experiences comes back to you in one form or another. At times we are treated poorly by others and we wonder why on earth someone would act in such a manner. Just know that in those moments, you always have a choice of how you want to respond. Just because they are putting bad karma out there (or what I like to call bad "juju") doesn't mean you have to put bad karma out there too.

You always have a choice in how you respond, even when it seems like you don't. It may seem difficult to change how you would normally respond by choosing to respond with love, especially when someone isn't treating you with love. But just remember, however you choose to react speaks volumes and is on its way back to you. Set you intention to change all your reactions of anger to responses of love! Just imagine all the good juju you'll be putting out there!

—✿ Empowered to A.C.T.: ✿—

What inspired **ACTION** will you take today?
What purposeful **CHANGE** will you make today?
What can you **TEACH** someone else today?

Happy Good Ju-Ju!

Remember, nothing happens until you decide to take action!

Be a Present Communicator

"The secret to being effective when you present to is stay present."
~ Bob Burg

Being present is so powerful! It allows you to absorb and process information that you otherwise would overlook and miss out on. Too often professionals get caught up in memorizing a script, elevator pitch, and presentation and they forget to be fully present for their audience because they're just reading off something memorized in their minds. Don't get me wrong—a script, an elevator pitch, and a presentation should be practiced and memorized; however, never leave out the REAL and AUTHENTIC YOU from those communications! The part of you that is truly curious about the other person, that wants to connect and be of great service and value to them, and the part of you that stays connected and grounded to the REAL and AUTHENTIC YOU! When you are present you share your greatest gift ... and that's YOU! How will you be more present in your conversations today?

⌐ Empowered to A.C.T.: ¬

What inspired **ACTION** will you take today?
What purposeful **CHANGE** will you make today?
What can you **TEACH** someone else today?

Happy Being a Present Communicator!

Remember, nothing happens until you decide to take action!

Embrace This Moment

"It's easy in a world of wild stimuli and omnipresent movement to forget to embrace life's enjoyable experiences. When we neglect to appreciate, we rob the moment of its magic."
~ Jacob Sensophy

In this day and age it can be very easy to get caught up in the day to day rat race. All of your physical senses are constantly being bombarded by television, advertisements, work, friends, family, etc. It can be very consuming and very quickly you may forget to "stop and smell the roses." Real happiness can only come when you slow down just enough to be present and really enjoy and savor the gifts of this present moment. This moment, right here right now, is calling for your attention. Take a few minutes right now to be present and give thanks for the blessings in your life. Allow happiness and gratitude to bubble up inside of you!

—ͻ Empowered to A.C.T.: ͻ—

What inspired **ACTION** will you take today?
What purposeful **CHANGE** will you make today?
What can you **TEACH** someone else today?

Happy Embracing This Moment!

Remember, nothing happens until you decide to take action!

Never Never Never Give Up!

"The greatest tragedy in the world is when the fire goes out in someone's eyes— when they give up, when they settle. Never let that happen to you."
~ Denise Ryan

No one is going to deny that at times things can get pretty challenging and you struggle to keep the fire within burning bright. It happens to the best of us. The goal here though is to never let giving up or settling even be an option. Sticking with something and keeping your fire burning bright is not always the easiest choice to make. Let's face it, sometimes giving up seems to be the easier of the two options. I'm inviting you not to do what's easy or comfortable; I'm inviting you to do what you need to do in order to keep your flame alive, to fulfill more of your potential, and to shine your brightest!

Empowered to A.C.T.:

What inspired **ACTION** will you take today?
What purposeful **CHANGE** will you make today?
What can you **TEACH** someone else today?

Happy Never Giving Up and Keeping Your FIRE Burning Bright!

Remember, nothing happens until you decide to take action!

Gratitude Rocks!

"Never let a day pass without looking for the good, feeling the good within you,
praising, appreciating, blessing, and being grateful. Make it your
life commitment, and you will stand in utter awe of what happens
in your life. May the joy be with you."
~ Rhonda Bryne

Gratitude can always save the day! When you're feeling overwhelmed, stressed out, and ready to throw in the towel, take a moment to take a nice deep breath and express some gratitude and appreciation for where you are here and now in your journey. On the surface it may appear to be less than ideal; however, if you look beyond the surface, you will find gifts and blessings that you can give thanks for. It will completely shift your perception! Unfortunately, personal and professional growth can be painful and messy at times, but growth wouldn't be growth without it.

Empowered to A.C.T.:

What inspired **ACTION** will you take today?
What purposeful **CHANGE** will you make today?
What can you **TEACH** someone else today?

Happy Giving Thanks for the Journey!

Remember, nothing happens until you decide to take action!

What is Real Family?

"Family isn't always blood. It's the people in your life who want you in theirs. The ones who accept you for who you are. The ones who would do anything to see you smile, and who love you no matter what."
~ Tim Sweeney

I love love love my family and a good majority of the wonderful people in my family aren't even biologically related to me! I have been blessed and honored to create beautiful connections worldwide and my heart is overflowing with love and gratitude. How about your family? Who is special in your life that accepts you, supports you, and encourages you to be your best? Look for those who believe in you, who love you no matter what. Blood related or not, that's family! Give thanks for those in your life who are your true family!

⟜ Empowered to A.C.T.: ⟞

What inspired **ACTION** will you take today?
What purposeful **CHANGE** will you make today?
What can you **TEACH** someone else today?

Happy Family!

Remember, nothing happens until you decide to take action!

Make The Message Your Own!

*"Reading furnishes the mind only with material and knowledge;
it is thinking that makes what we read ours."*
~ John Locke

Don't read just for the sake of reading. Read to absorb the message and make it personal and your own. When I read a book, I like to read the book as if the author was talking to me personally. I think to myself, "What's the author trying to tell me?" and "What message is here for me?" Each of us may be receiving a different message from the same book and that's OK. The point is that you receive the message you were meant to receive and you do something with it. That message wasn't delivered to you for no reason. Make it your own by doing something with it that will improve your life and the life of others.

⚬ Empowered to A.C.T.: ⚬

What inspired **ACTION** will you take today?
What purposeful **CHANGE** will you make today?
What can you **TEACH** someone else today?

Happy Making the Message Your Own!

Remember, nothing happens until you decide to take action!

Be Conscious of Your Treasures!

"We can only be said to be alive in those moments
when our hearts are conscious of our treasures."
~ Thornton Wilder

Make the commitment to take time every day to acknowledge and give thanks for the treasures that are not only in your life, but also in your heart and soul; they were given to you for a great purpose. Sometimes I think it's easier for us to give thanks for the food on our tables and clothes on our backs than it is to give thanks for the purpose of our life and our magnificent human spirit and mind. See the great purpose your life has. See the treasures in your heart such as love, patience, kindness, gratitude and compassion. These are priceless treasures that we must recognize are within us. Give thanks to your creator for placing them in your heart. Now it's your job to glorify them and live FROM them.

Empowered to A.C.T.:

What inspired **ACTION** will you take today?
What purposeful **CHANGE** will you make today?
What can you **TEACH** someone else today?

Happy Glorifying the Treasures in Your Heart!

Remember, nothing happens until you decide to take action!

Are You a Good Decision Maker?

"Achieving your goals is NOT a problem of goal setting.
We are goal setting experts. Goal achieving is an issue of
continuous and consistent decision making."
~ Unknown

As we set new goals, we ignite the excitement and anticipation of upcoming achievements and creations. One minor, yet major, detail that we seem to overlook is strengthening our decision making skills. You see, in order to actually keep your goals alive and actually achieve them, you must make a committed decision to create them. This means you are totally committed to consistently and continuously making choices that are congruent with the achievement of your desired goal. So as you sit down and write out your goals for the month and quarter ahead, be sure to establish a meaningful and unwavering commitment to them. Reignite your intention and commitment to your desired goals every morning and night!

⁓ Empowered to A.C.T.: ⁓

What inspired **ACTION** will you take today?
What purposeful **CHANGE** will you make today?
What can you **TEACH** someone else today?

Happy Total Commitment to Your Goals!

Remember, nothing happens until you decide to take action!

How Do You Show Up?

"Draw the chin in, carry the crown of the head high, and fill the lungs to the
utmost; drink in the sunshine; greet your friends with a smile,
and put soul into every handclasp."
~ Elbert Hubbard

How do you show up in life? Who are you really being in your business? In your
relationships? And how about when you greet the morning sun? Are you being
your best self or your grumpy, tired self? Acknowledge that the dominating energy
that resides inside of you is backing your every thought and move and is having a
huge impact on your results.

Empowered to A.C.T.:

What inspired **ACTION** will you take today?
What purposeful **CHANGE** will you make today?
What can you **TEACH** someone else today?

Happy Showing Up With Your Best Self!

Remember, nothing happens until you decide to take action!

LOVE Your Excellence!

"The sad truth is that EXCELLENCE makes people nervous."
~ Shana Alexander

Your excellence and magnificence is an amazing and wonderful thing, so why does it make so many people nervous? I say shout it from the mountain tops! I believe there are two main reasons why excellence makes some people nervous. One: some people have been taught to believe they are less than so when they start doing excellent things, it's not in harmony with their current limiting belief system. It gives them an uncomfortable feeling so they reject it and don't believe they could maintain it, let alone that they really deserve it. Two: many people are afraid of finding out what they are really capable of because then it might shine a light on their true power and they'll see how much they've been settling for and not living up to their full potential. They would rather hide from their excellence than work on developing it; the good ole avoidance tactic! If one of these reasons applies to you, seek to embrace your excellence, not ignore or avoid it. Be willing to do the inner and outer work necessary to break free from these fears and LOVE YOUR EXCELLENCE!

⟶ Empowered to A.C.T.: ⟵

What inspired **ACTION** will you take today?
What purposeful **CHANGE** will you make today?
What can you **TEACH** someone else today?

Happy Loving Your Excellence!

Remember, nothing happens until you decide to take action!

Do You Have a Healthy Self-Esteem?

"Having a healthy self-esteem is the greatest protection against those who enjoy breaking other people's dreams."
~ Carla Cunningham

Many people are easily influenced by others when it comes to creating their dreams. So often I see people giving up on their dreams simply because someone else doesn't believe in them. We must hold on tight to our dreams and never ever give up on them! You may be thinking that that is easier said than done. Well, the healthier your self-esteem and self-confidence are, the more likely you are not going to give in to those negative outside influences. You will believe in yourself and you will listen and be guided by your heart and purpose. I remember early on in my career change I wasn't supported the way I had hoped for. However, every cell in my body knew this was the right change for me and therefore I never gave up on my dream!

—⟡ Empowered to A.C.T.: ⟡—

What inspired **ACTION** will you take today?
What purposeful **CHANGE** will you make today?
What can you **TEACH** someone else today?

Happy Living the Dream, My Friends!

Remember, nothing happens until you decide to take action!

119

Stop Complaining!

"If you don't like something, change it. If you can't change it,
change your attitude. Don't complain."
~ Maya Angelou

If you think about it, within every complaint is a request. When someone is complaining, they are really just requesting change. They want things to be different. At that point, whether it's yourself complaining or someone else, take a moment and dig out the request. Identify if it's something you can actually change and do something about and of course, if you can do something about it, then get moving! If it is out of your hands and it's something you cannot necessarily change, then stop wasting your precious time and energy when you could be putting it to better use. Redirect your focus onto what you do have the control to change and then get started!

— Empowered to A.C.T.: —

What inspired **ACTION** will you take today?
What purposeful **CHANGE** will you make today?
What can you **TEACH** someone else today?

Happy Changing What You Can Change!

Remember, nothing happens until you decide to take action!

Celebrate Who You Are!

"Stop focusing on what you can't be and start celebrating who you are."
~ Denise Ryan

Do you ever get frustrated when you spend time and energy watching others doing extraordinary things and you begin to wonder if there is something you are lacking? You may see professional athletes breaking records, actors winning awards, and business products changing the world. At times it can be easy to get caught up in some self-judgment when comparing yourself to what these types of people are doing and creating. Here's the deal … THEY DON'T HAVE ANYTHING WITHIN THEM THAT YOU DON'T HAVE! They are simply expressing and sharing their gifts and talents with the world! You have been gifted with your very own special gifts and talents that are meant to break records, win awards, and change the world too. It may not be a sport, movie, or product, but indeed your mere existence tells me that you were put here for a very special purpose. Celebrate your purpose! Celebrate YOU! How can you acknowledge and celebrate more of your uniqueness today?

― Empowered to A.C.T.: ―

What inspired **ACTION** will you take today?
What purposeful **CHANGE** will you make today?
What can you **TEACH** someone else today?

Happy Celebrating YOU!

Remember, nothing happens until you decide to take action!

Make the Most of Every Moment

"Life is like a taxi. The meter just keeps a-ticking whether you
are getting somewhere or just standing still."
~ Lou Erickson

Are you making the most of every moment in your life? You see, time doesn't stop
and wait for you to get in a good mood to do something positive and productive
with your life, but rather time keeps on a-ticking regardless of your mood or
opinion of it and you just end up paying the high price for doing so. It's up to you
to get real present and take advantage of every second life has to offer you. The
journey becomes much more beautiful when you're actually going places in life.
What will you do with today's moments? Will you savor each one or will you let
them pass you by? The choice is yours. Be happy savoring the moments!

⚘ Empowered to A.C.T.: ⚘

What inspired **ACTION** will you take today?
What purposeful **CHANGE** will you make today?
What can you **TEACH** someone else today?

Happy Believing in the Unseen!

Remember, nothing happens until you decide to take action!

Do You Believe in Your Dream?

"The future belongs to those who believe in the beauty of their dreams."
~ Eleanor Roosevelt

Do you believe in your dreams? Many people wish and hope for their dreams to come true; however, they don't really BELIEVE or EXPECT them to come true. They are projecting mixed energy signals. "Yes, I want it, but I don't believe in it." Yes, no, maybe so … Talk about confusing! Be very clear on your dreams and believe and expect with all your heart that they will come to fruition. Fall in love with them! See the beauty in them! The alternative is not to believe and not to expect your dreams to come true. We all know that is no way to live! Your dreams are waiting for you to believe in them. What are you waiting for?

⟶ Empowered to A.C.T.: ⟵

What inspired **ACTION** will you take today?
What purposeful **CHANGE** will you make today?
What can you **TEACH** someone else today?

Happy Believing and Expecting Your Dreams to Come True!

Remember, nothing happens until you decide to take action!

When Was The Last Time You Expressed Gratitude?

"Silent gratitude isn't much use to anyone."
~ G.B. Stern

Who and what are you grateful for? Have you expressed that gratitude lately? If yes, keep it up because it's so powerful and makes such a significant and positive impact in yours and others' lives. If not, then the time is NOW! There is no reason to keep gratitude to yourself. EXPRESS IT, SHARE IT! Make a list of people and things you are grateful for and express and share your gratitude. The more you do this, the more you significantly lift others and yourself up!

── Empowered to A.C.T.: ──

What inspired **ACTION** will you take today?
What purposeful **CHANGE** will you make today?
What can you **TEACH** someone else today?

Happy Expressing Gratitude!

Remember, nothing happens until you decide to take action!

What Do You Believe In?

"I believe in sunshine, fresh air, friendship, calm sleep,
and beautiful thoughts."
~ Elbert Hubbard

I believe in all these things too! I love them all! I also believe in people, big
dreams, true love, and experiences that make my heart smile. I believe in reading
a book that's so good I can't put it down, listening to music that makes me get
out of my seat, and being around friends who feel like family. I BELIEVE IN THE
POWER OF LOVING LIFE! Boy, oh, boy, do I love life! What do you believe in
that makes you feel oooh oooh so good? Jot down five things that you can't help
but love believing in!

⟶ Empowered to A.C.T.: ⟵

What inspired **ACTION** will you take today?
What purposeful **CHANGE** will you make today?
What can you **TEACH** someone else today?

Happy Believing!

Remember, nothing happens until you decide to take action!

Create the Non-Existent

"By believing passionately in something that does not exist, we create it. The non-existent is whatever we have not sufficiently desired."
~ Nikos Kazantzakis

Do you have a burning desire to be, do, or have something in your life that doesn't currently exist? Maybe it's something that seems impossible. Well, guess what? You can create it … IF you sufficiently desire it! Ever have a great goal, but abandon it before it came to fruition? That just means you didn't sufficiently desire that goal. When you sufficiently desire something that means you stick with it, you focus on it, and you take massive action on it. You relish in the possibility of it and you take steps in the direction of creating it! The more you do this, the more the right resources, the right answers and guidance will all come to you in the perfect time, sequence and space. Remember, your thoughts are things! They carry creative energy. Be sure your thoughts, feelings and actions are all in alignment! You can create the non-existent, my friend!

⟿ Empowered to A.C.T.: ⟿

What inspired **ACTION** will you take today?
What purposeful **CHANGE** will you make today?
What can you **TEACH** someone else today?

Happy Creating the Non-Existent!

Remember, nothing happens until you decide to take action!

Burning Desire and Skill Are a Must!

"When love and skill work together, expect a masterpiece."
~ Sharon Gunning

Don't you just love when you combine your burning desire and passion with your skillsets and talent! Amazing things happen, don't they?! I'm such a huge advocate of doing what you love and loving what you're doing! Listen to and follow your heart; it will lead you to your true calling and purpose in life. You will maximize your purpose in life by developing and mastering your greatest talents and skill sets. Combine your burning desire and mastered skills and talents and in no time your purpose will become your reality. You will be surrounded by masterpieces. Plus, life is just so much more fun, yummy and delicious when you're living a purpose-driven life!

Remember, nothing happens until you decide to take action!

⌁ Empowered to A.C.T.: ⌁

What inspired **ACTION** will you take today?
What purposeful **CHANGE** will you make today?
What can you **TEACH** someone else today?

Happy Purpose Driven Life!

Remember, nothing happens until you decide to take action!

Today's Featured Reader:
Trent S. White, Thayne, Wyoming
"I have always loved the word desire, because success starts here in my opinion. Melissa, thank you for your efforts in reaching people through your words of wisdom."

We All Benefit From Your Growth!

"As your life presents new problems, it also presents new solutions, which cause expansion—and all-that-is benefits from your willingness to live and consider and explore ... and expand."
~ Esther Hicks (Teachings of Abraham)

Think about how your expansion and growth benefits EVERYTHING, all-that-is. Without your willingness to live life to the fullest, everything and everyone else suffers! Just imagine what we miss out on when people focus on problems and don't follow through on their true calling, give up, and quit! It's a shame to see all that LIFE and POTENTIAL go untapped and wasted! You have a very important role in this world and it's so important to all of us that you grow and expand into your greatest, most authentic self. It's your willingness to face roadblocks, challenges, and keep forging ahead that benefits not just you, but everyone and everything! YOU impact mankind!

—◦ Empowered to A.C.T.: ◦—

What inspired **ACTION** will you take today?
What purposeful **CHANGE** will you make today?
What can you **TEACH** someone else today?

Happy Growth and Expansion!

Remember, nothing happens until you decide to take action!

BE Your Best and You'll Do Your Best!

"Fulfillment could never be in your doing; only in your being."
~ Unknown

It's not so much the actual activity that you enjoy or don't enjoy, it's who you are BEING while you are doing that activity that makes you enjoy or not enjoy it. There may be activities you love, but there are always those times here and there that you don't enjoy it as much and it seems like "work" to you. You see, the activity itself didn't change, just how you showed up; who you were BEING is all that changed. Think about how you show up and who you are being in your career, in your relationships with others as well as the relationship with yourself, and in everything you do from the minute you wake up until the minute you go to bed.

⟶ Empowered to A.C.T.: ⟵

What inspired **ACTION** will you take today?
What purposeful **CHANGE** will you make today?
What can you **TEACH** someone else today?

Happy BEING Your Best You!

Remember, nothing happens until you decide to take action!

Want to Be Great?

"The way I like to measure greatness is ...
How many people can you make want to be better?"
~ Will Smith

Do you want to help others be a better version of themselves? I believe there is a part of all of us that strives to make the world a better place by bringing out the greatness in people. When you connect to your deeper and greater purpose of wanting to help others and you set your intention to change lives and bring out the greatness in people, guess what? Your own greatness is magnified! Your greatest self shines even brighter! It's totally a WIN-WIN for everyone all around! So what are you waiting for? Go help someone BE amazing today!

 Empowered to A.C.T.:

What inspired **ACTION** will you take today?
What purposeful **CHANGE** will you make today?
What can you **TEACH** someone else today?

Happy Bringing Out the Greatness in Others and YOURSELF!

Remember, nothing happens until you decide to take action!

May

Stand Up Again and Again!

"Fall seven times, stand up eight."
~ Japanese Proverb

Ouch! Falling can be painful, can't it? But actually, it hurts even more to stay fallen than it does to get up! As difficult and painful as it may seem to get back up again after a hard fall, it's such an important part of our journey and transformation. We learn and grow so much from dusting ourselves off and standing back up again. We are stronger, more aware, more experienced, and wiser! Where have you fallen? What did you learn about yourself and life in general from getting back up? A lot I'm sure! Where have you fallen and not yet gotten back up? It's time to stand up, my friend … I believe in you!

⁓ Empowered to A.C.T.: ⁓

What inspired **ACTION** will you take today?
What purposeful **CHANGE** will you make today?
What can you **TEACH** someone else today?

Happy Standing Tall and Strong!

Remember, nothing happens until you decide to take action!

Live Your Life by Design

"It's not what happens to you. It's what you do about it."
~ W. Mitchell

We all have things happen to us in life that are less than ideal. The goal isn't to try and eliminate these experiences, but rather to grow from them and alter our response to them. W. Mitchell is an amazing man who survived a blazing motorcycle accident and a paralyzing plane crash. He has such a powerful message about taking responsibility for your life and successfully overcoming impossible situations. The time is now for you to grow from all that you have experienced and create a life by design rather than by default. Don't let life happen TO YOU, but rather go out there and create and design the life you wish you live. In order to do so, you must GROW! What are you going to do to grow from where you are today to where you want to be tomorrow?

Empowered to A.C.T.:

What inspired **ACTION** will you take today?
What purposeful **CHANGE** will you make today?
What can you **TEACH** someone else today?

Happy Designing Your Life!

Remember, nothing happens until you decide to take action!

MAY 3ᴿᴰ

Lead With Authenticity!

"Great leaders don't try to be perfect, they try to be themselves.
And that's what makes them great."
~ Simon Sinek

Too often I see people trying to be someone they are not and that's a miserable way to live. Be YOURSELF ... your true and authentic self! Longevity in leadership is built on many things, authenticity being at the top if the list. I feel like those who are phony wanna-be leaders are only fooling themselves. They are the ones who are truly missing out on creating something real, fulfilling, and purposeful in their lives. They are missing out on sharing their greatest gift ... themselves! Wouldn't you agree that you are most inspired to follow those who are authentic and genuine? Choose to be authentic and genuine in your leadership and you will have the foundation for being a great leader!

Empowered to A.C.T.:

What inspired **ACTION** will you take today?
What purposeful **CHANGE** will you make today?
What can you **TEACH** someone else today?

Happy Authentic Leadership!

Remember, nothing happens until you decide to take action!

Being Present

"Life is too short, so kiss slowly, laugh insanely,
love truly, and forgive quickly."
~ Unknown

Life is waaaay too short to miss out on enjoying those precious moments that can be so easily missed if we're not paying attention. Think of the times you are with your dear friends and family, the smiles on your loved ones' faces, the belly-aching laughs, the breathtaking views of nature, the moments that teach you a huge lesson by knocking you down and taking your breath away! I believe each and every moment we have is precious and a once-in-a-lifetime moment. We get that moment once and we can never get it back again. I encourage you to take the time today to BE IN THE MOMENT and SAVOR IT! Be present and be open to receiving the gifts that every moment has to offer that will help you continually move forward.

— Empowered to A.C.T.: —

What inspired **ACTION** will you take today?
What purposeful **CHANGE** will you make today?
What can you **TEACH** someone else today?

Happy Moments!

Remember, nothing happens until you decide to take action!

Trust the Process

"The word patience means the willingness to stay where we are and live the situation out to the fullest in the belief that something hidden there will manifest itself to us."
~ Henri J.M. Nouwen

Patience is about TRUST. It's trusting in the process of achievement. Most of us don't like to wait on our goals and dreams to come to fruition. We would soooo rather have them be here today! However, just like farmers must trust that if they water and nurture their seeds, that in the perfect time, that crop will break through the ground and be ready for harvest. You too must be willing to be patient when there is no physical evidence of the manifestation of your goals. Your job is to hold your vision and stay true to your goals and what you say you desire in life. Take purposeful and inspired action every day in the direction of your goals, with or without the evidence.

⸺◦ Empowered to A.C.T.: ◦⸺

What inspired **ACTION** will you take today?
What purposeful **CHANGE** will you make today?
What can you **TEACH** someone else today?

Happy Trusting the Process!

Remember, nothing happens until you decide to take action!

Express Gratitude and Appreciation TODAY!

*"The only people with whom you should try to get even with
are those who have helped you."*
~ John E. Southard

There are so many people in your life who have helped you out in one way or another. Have you taken the time to express your appreciation and gratitude? I don't believe when you do good things for other people that you do it expecting something nice in return; however, you have to admit, when you do something gracious for someone and they express their appreciation and gratitude it feels simply wonderful. It actually makes you want to do it over and over again. Take 10 minutes today to think of five or more people that have helped you in the past that you have not had a chance to express your appreciation and gratitude to yet. Write them a hand written note, call them, email them, or take them out to lunch. Whatever it is, let them know that you appreciate them and their help.

— Empowered to A.C.T.: —

What inspired **ACTION** will you take today?
What purposeful **CHANGE** will you make today?
What can you **TEACH** someone else today?

Happy Expressing Appreciation and Gratitude!

Remember, nothing happens until you decide to take action!

Do You Ooze Love?

"If you meditate deeply, sooner or later you will start feeling tremendous love arising in you that you have never known before. You want a love which is born out of meditation, not born out of the mind."

~ Osho

Meditation is a great way to feel and experience love with ease. Find 10-15 minutes in your day where you can be still and clear your mind. Breathe into your heart space and stir up the love that's there in your heart. Feel the love you have for all the amazing blessings in your life. It could be the love you have for your loved ones, your health, the view out your window, your smile, the warm sunshine on your face, and so on. Really allow yourself to FEEL the love bubble up from within you. When you do, you will just naturally express it and share it with others. Focus on that feeling and before you know it, you'll be oozing love!

— Empowered to A.C.T.: —

What inspired **ACTION** will you take today?
What purposeful **CHANGE** will you make today?
What can you **TEACH** someone else today?

Happy Oozing Love!

Remember, nothing happens until you decide to take action!

Think Before You Choose!

"Everything in life is a choice. Every choice comes with a consequence, good or bad. Think before you choose your consequence."
~ Unknown

In every moment of your day you have a choice to make. Each one of those choices creates an impact. Sometimes the impact is good and serves you and others well and sometimes the impact is bad and is a disservice to you and others. Before you take action, consider the impact. Ask yourself if the choice you are about to make is going to energize, inspire and lift you and others up or is it going to drain you and drag you and others down? Make choices that bring the best out of you and others. As you go through the day, stop and check in with yourself and see how you are doing. See what kind of choices you are making. I guarantee you, you'll make better choices in life just by being more conscious and deliberate about the choices you are making!

— Empowered to A.C.T.: —

What inspired **ACTION** will you take today?
What purposeful **CHANGE** will you make today?
What can you **TEACH** someone else today?

Happy Making Conscious Choices!

Remember, nothing happens until you decide to take action!

Get Out of Your Head!

"Business is an art, which you can master if you
work from the heart and work with love."
~ Venus

Do you ever get caught in your head when it comes to running your business and/
or in your career? Sometimes I get caught in my head and I forget to let my heart
lead the way. It is imperative in your career and in your personal life that you
involve your heart and soul and let it lead the way. You won't master business or
success in any area of your life without it. Can you name one massively successful
person who has maintained their success and continues to expand their business
and message that isn't working from their heart and coming from a place of
passion and love? NOPE! Those who are massively successful OOZE passion and
love for what they do and the people they serve.

—◦ Empowered to A.C.T.: ◦—

What inspired **ACTION** will you take today?
What purposeful **CHANGE** will you make today?
What can you **TEACH** someone else today?

Happy Getting Out of Your Head and Into Your Heart!

Remember, nothing happens until you decide to take action!

What is the Bridge to Success?

"Discipline is the bridge between goals and accomplishment."
~ Owen Waters

I think many people try to force themselves to be disciplined. They arm wrestle themselves to the ground to stick with something. Is it really necessary that discipline be so grueling and unpleasant? I believe a more enjoyable way to be disciplined isn't through force, but rather through building up your faith and focus. Take time to believe in the unseen and develop your ability to stay focused on it. You want your focus to be on the possibilities and not on fear and lack. When you are in a state of belief of your possibilities, you will naturally take aligned and inspired action. It will seem effortless! However, as soon as your attention strays, there goes your discipline. Stay focused, my friend!

⁓ Empowered to A.C.T.: ⁓

What inspired **ACTION** will you take today?
What purposeful **CHANGE** will you make today?
What can you **TEACH** someone else today?

Happy Building your Faith and Focus!

Remember, nothing happens until you decide to take action!

Today's Featured Reader:
Mark Hernandez, Baytown, Texas
"This quote and your words of wisdom have impacted me so much that I have decided to be intentional and not only write a goal down on paper, but live it out to completion. What began as just a thought of writing content for a Purpose, Vision, and Goals workshop turned into 92 hours of work to complete the content and it has now been delivered and positively impacted over 250 people. Thank you Melissa!"

Who Should You Be?

"What ought a man be? Well, my short answer is—himself."
~ Henrik Ibsen

Many people look outside themselves when they ask the question, "Who should I be? What should I do?" I suggest asking that question from within. The answer is always always always to be YOU, but then the next question is, "Who are you?" What makes you "you"? What inspires and motivates you? What are you drawn to that lifts your soul up? If you are going to be your best you, you must know what people, environments, tasks, projects, draw out your best you. Take some time today to contemplate those questions. Then, from your answers, make decisions and choices that honor and are in alignment with you being your best you. The great thing about you being your best you is that not only do you feel awesome energy; others feel it as well because they are getting your best stuff! Wow, what a great gift to give yourself and others!

—◦ Empowered to A.C.T.: ◦—

What inspired **ACTION** will you take today?
What purposeful **CHANGE** will you make today?
What can you **TEACH** someone else today?

Happy Being YOU!

Remember, nothing happens until you decide to take action!

Share Your Story!

"You have an entire story to tell and no one can tell it quite like you."
~ Byron Embry

Your life is full of lessons, experiences, good and bad, and behind all of them there is a powerful message, a powerful story you are meant to share with the world that will leave an imprint and change lives forever. Don't think for a second that your message isn't worth sharing! You are meant to share it ... whether it's with your kids, a co-worker, or a large audience! The other day I did a presentation on my journey thus far in life and I shared how I've overcome some of my life challenges. I didn't think it was one of my better presentations, so I was pleasantly surprised when afterward one of the attendees came up to me and told me how much they were impacted and inspired by my story. My story had a message and she was meant to hear it. You too have a story and a message that others need to hear. Share it!

Remember, nothing happens until you decide to take action!

⟶ Empowered to A.C.T.: ⟵

What inspired **ACTION** will you take today?
What purposeful **CHANGE** will you make today?
What can you **TEACH** someone else today?

Happy Sharing Your Story!

Remember, nothing happens until you decide to take action!

Roll Up Those Sleeves!

"Genius is one percent inspiration and ninety-nine percent perspiration."
~ Thomas Edison

We all get inspired, right? You and I may not be inspired by the same things, yet something that displays the beauty and strength of the human spirit is usually very inspiring to us all. The real question is, what do you do with your inspiration? Do you take action and create something amazing from it even if you have to grow to create it? Or do you let it die before it even has a chance just because you don't have all the answers? Inspiration never acted upon remains an aspiration. It's something you aspire to act upon one day, but you never do anything with it; it remains a hope and a wish. Roll up your sleeves today and put some blood, sweat, and tears into creating your heart's greatest desires! You are a genius after all, right? So get to work, my friend!

Remember, nothing happens until you decide to take action!

—◦ Empowered to A.C.T.: ◦—

What inspired **ACTION** will you take today?
What purposeful **CHANGE** will you make today?
What can you **TEACH** someone else today?

Happy Genius!

Remember, nothing happens until you decide to take action!

LOL! LOL! LOL! :)

"Laugh often, a lot and long. Laugh until you gasp for breath. And if you have a friend who makes you laugh, spend lots and lots of time with them."
~ Unknown

I love love love .... love love to LAUGH! Laughing at hilarious jokes, at myself blending my morning shake with no cover on the blender, falling out of my car, watching funny YouTube vids such as Brian Reagan's comedy show, chatting with friends about old times as someone trips up the stairs (sorry, can't help it!), at my silly nephews and niece just being kids ... and on and on. I mean come on, we live in a pretty hilarious world! If you're not laughing at least three times a day, you need to come over and hang out with me some more! If you can't make it over, at least find one of those funny animal videos on YouTube or something. Turn that frown upside down and give me a SMILE and LAUGH!

— Empowered to A.C.T.: —

What inspired **ACTION** will you take today?
What purposeful **CHANGE** will you make today?
What can you **TEACH** someone else today?

Happy Exercising Those Laughing Muscles!

Remember, nothing happens until you decide to take action!

How Do You Become Authentic?

"How do I become authentic? The truth is, authentic is not something you become; It's something you already are. Authenticity is not something you seek or take on, it's something you simply embrace."
~ Bob Burg

Do you embrace your authenticity? See that there is more value in you being the real you than there is in you pretending to be someone you are not. See that YOU are the gift; YOU are special and magnificent and have a lot to offer this world! If you can't see that value, it will be very difficult to embrace it. I believe that when you are operating from a place of authenticity you are in a natural state of love, kindness, curiosity, playfulness, and happiness. At your core, that is your natural state. It's not something you force or pretend. Look at a baby, a baby doesn't need to pretend to be loving, kind, curious, playful or happy. They just naturally are ... and SO ARE YOU! Embrace it!

—◦ Empowered to A.C.T.: ◦—

What inspired **ACTION** will you take today?
What purposeful **CHANGE** will you make today?
What can you **TEACH** someone else today?

Happy Embracing Your Authentic You!

Remember, nothing happens until you decide to take action!

Breathe... Ahhhhh Yessss!

"The process of breathing is much more than an essential function of your physical body. Indeed, it is the flowing of Spirit to you, and through you."
~ Esther Hicks (Teachings of Abraham)

Breathing is soooo underrated! When you take nice deep cleansing breaths you cause an interruption in your mind chatter and you create a moment of opportunity to be present and aware of the Spirit moving to, with, and through you. You will feel the Spirit within guiding you and helping you navigate through life. Your job is to stay present and connected to it as much as possible. You see, all the answers are already within you. If you guide your awareness to the Spirit within, you will feel your strength within, rather than your weakness. Make it a regular practice throughout your day to take nice deep breaths and be aware of the Spirit within. Trust it! Follow it!

—❧ Empowered to A.C.T.: ☙—

What inspired **ACTION** will you take today?
What purposeful **CHANGE** will you make today?
What can you **TEACH** someone else today?

Happy Breathing! Ahhhhhhh Yessssss!

Remember, nothing happens until you decide to take action!

It's Really Just Feedback

"When defeat comes, accept it as a signal that your plans are not sound, rebuild those plans, and set sail once more toward your coveted goal."
~ Napoleon Hill

Many people fear defeat, but really defeat is just feedback. It just lets you know that an adjustment is needed. It's not a sign to quit! Choose to keep your desired goal alive and see it as an opportunity to assess, reflect, gain order, put a plan together and take another shot at it. You'll never know what could have been if you don't give it another shot! Take that chance on yourself, face your fears, and KNOW in your heart of hearts that you truly can CREATE whatever you wish if you are willing to take forward action.

Empowered to A.C.T.:

What inspired **ACTION** will you take today?
What purposeful **CHANGE** will you make today?
What can you **TEACH** someone else today?

Happy Feedback!

Remember, nothing happens until you decide to take action!

Be Determined Every Morning

"You've got to get up every morning with determination
if you're going to go to bed with satisfaction."
~ George Lorimer

How do you feel each night when your head hits the pillow? Are you satisfied with the day you created? Consistently each day I wake up with gratitude! Some days are harder than others, but gratitude has never failed me, it always motivates me and feeds my determination. I know that if I don't intentionally get into a state of gratitude I will have a hard time being motivated and determined to take on the day and create something purposeful and amazing. I have a great desire to end my days with tremendous fulfillment and satisfaction. I don't know about you, but I sleep better too! Gratitude has become a daily practice for me. How about you? How could you use gratitude to help get stay motivated and determined to create a successful and fulfilling day?

— Empowered to A.C.T.: —

What inspired **ACTION** will you take today?
What purposeful **CHANGE** will you make today?
What can you **TEACH** someone else today?

Happy Using Gratitude to Stay Determined!

Remember, nothing happens until you decide to take action!

What Are Your Emotions Telling You?

"The walls we build around us to keep out sadness,
but they also keep out the joy."
~ Jim Rohn

When you build walls around you, you basically numb yourself from feeling your emotions ... the bad feeling ones AND the good feeling ones. In an attempt to "protect" yourself from feeling the bad emotions, you rob yourself of being able to experience real joy and happiness too. It may feel too vulnerable to open yourself, so you don't, you stay closed off and "protected," missing out on the great joys of life. As much as sadness may not be a desired emotion, it actually has a purpose. It comes with a message, a lesson, and a gift ... as does every emotion. Instead of avoiding and running from the bad feeling emotions, open yourself up to all emotions. Learn from your emotions. Learn more about yourself and about life. What if there was a message in every emotion? What are your emotions telling you? Perhaps there is good reason to let those walls around you fall.

— Empowered to A.C.T.: —

What inspired **ACTION** will you take today?
What purposeful **CHANGE** will you make today?
What can you **TEACH** someone else today?

Happy Learning From Your Emotions!

Remember, nothing happens until you decide to take action!

151

Where Do You Invest Your Energy?

"You've done it before and you can do it now. See the positive possibilities. Redirect the substantial energy of your frustration and turn it into positive, effective, and unstoppable determination."

~ Ralph Marston

Have you ever wondered how you were going to make it through a difficult time? I'm sure we have all had those thoughts at one time or another, right? The real question becomes, how did you respond to your own doubt? Did you focus on your strengths and abilities or your limitations and the barriers? Remember, you are ALWAYS greater than any problem you face ... as long as you think you are. The minute you think you are smaller is when you run into more problems. Now is the time to stop questioning yourself and believe in your strengths, abilities and resourcefulness! Where will you direct your energy today?

⟶ Empowered to A.C.T.: ∾

What inspired **ACTION** will you take today?
What purposeful **CHANGE** will you make today?
What can you **TEACH** someone else today?

Happy Directing!

Remember, nothing happens until you decide to take action!

What's Your Life's Purpose?

"I believe each of us is born with a life purpose. Identifying, acknowledging, and honoring this purpose is perhaps the most important action successful people take."
~ Jack Canfield

Ahhh, purpose! It's one of those things I can't stop talking about. It is my purpose to help you identify, acknowledge, and honor your own purpose; to know who you are and to live it and breathe it every day, to find the purpose in everything you do from the minute you wake up to the minute you go to bed. I invite you to know that everything you do has great purpose and significance. Do you feel a great sense of purpose throughout every minute of your day? If not, would you like to? It'll require some self-reflection, but it will be well worth your time and effort! Before you do anything today, yes anything, I invite you to ask yourself "WHY am I doing this? WHY do I want this? What are the greater reasons for me doing or wanting this?" Seek the greater reason behind every choice you make today. Begin to understand the greater purpose that drives you. A little clue about knowing if you found your purpose or not is whether or not it emotionally moves you.

— Empowered to A.C.T.: —

What inspired **ACTION** will you take today?
What purposeful **CHANGE** will you make today?
What can you **TEACH** someone else today?

Happy Living a Purpose Filled Life!

Remember, nothing happens until you decide to take action!

Read the Good Stuff!

"Don't just read the easy stuff. You may be entertained by it,
but you will never grow from it."
~ Jim Rohn

I love love love to read great books that make me think and evolve past my current
level of thinking and knowledge! What have you read lately that gave you a new
perspective, challenged your current thinking, shed some light on an interesting
idea or topic? It's so important for us to be plugged into something which
accomplishes this. What are you plugged into? Make a commitment to yourself
to read at least 30 minutes per day. I love audio books too, so maybe you prefer
listening to a book? Audio books make for great traveling companions on long or
short commutes!

 Empowered to A.C.T.:

What inspired **ACTION** will you take today?
What purposeful **CHANGE** will you make today?
What can you **TEACH** someone else today?

Happy Reading the Good Stuff!

Remember, nothing happens until you decide to take action!

Passionately Love What You Love!

"The heart that truly loves never forgets."
~ Proverb

Think about what your heart truly loves to love. What does your heart love so much that you are willing to commit your life to it? Is it your family, your career, your community, a greater cause, and maybe even your country? Whatever it is, see how much your heart ignites and shines bright when you just think about it. The type of energy that the heart generates is incredible. I always say that when you fall in love with something your willingness to take action and take risks skyrockets. Love will make you go the extra mile, bend over backwards, and do whatever is necessary to make something work out. That kind of love is not forgotten!

⁓ Empowered to A.C.T.: ⁓

What inspired **ACTION** will you take today?
What purposeful **CHANGE** will you make today?
What can you **TEACH** someone else today?

Happy Passionately Loving What You Love!

Remember, nothing happens until you decide to take action!

Change From the Inside Out!

"Always do your best. What you plant now, you will harvest later."
~ Og Mandino

The thoughts, feelings, and actions you take now determine what you create in your life. Think about it ... really think about what you are "planting." If you want to know what you have been planting up until this point, take a look at your current results. The current results you are getting in your life are a reflection of what thoughts, feelings, and actions you have been having. If you see something you would like to change, begin to entertain some new thoughts, ideas, give it a new meaning, tell a new story, and have a new perspective about that situation. Until you change what's going on inside, you won't see changes on the outside. Remember, nothing happens until you decide to take action! Reflect on a situation that you now have a new perspective on.

— Empowered to A.C.T.: —

What inspired **ACTION** will you take today?
What purposeful **CHANGE** will you make today?
What can you **TEACH** someone else today?

Happy Changing From the Inside Out!

Remember, nothing happens until you decide to take action!

Are You Settling?

"If the majority of your days are not days where you are ready to disturb
the world in pursuit of whatever it is you want (your goals)
then you are settling for mediocrity."
~ Unknown

Think about it … how do you wake up? How do you spend your days? Are you
settling or are you in pursuit of fulfilling your goals and creating your vision? Are
you actively changing the world and making a positive impact or are you just
thinking about it and talking about it? Stop just thinking about it and talking about
it and actually go out there and claim an extraordinary life for yourself! Your actions
speak volumes! Yes, it requires you to reach, stretch, and grow in order to do so, but
I guarantee you, it'll be well worth it! Don't settle for mediocrity, my friend!

—◌ Empowered to A.C.T.: ◌—

What inspired **ACTION** will you take today?
What purposeful **CHANGE** will you make today?
What can you **TEACH** someone else today?

Happy Creating an Extraordinary Life!

Remember, nothing happens until you decide to take action!

157

Life Is Fun!

"Life is meant to be fun and abundant. This is your truth!"
~ David Childerley

One of my favorite colleagues, Tracey G., is so great to work with because she oozes FUN! She's always in a fabulous mood and seeks to bring fun and joy into everything she does. She has a playful spirit and has great energy that makes me want to be around her. How fun is your life? Is it time to have a fun makeover and spice up your environment a little bit? My challenge to you today is to find a way to add more fun and abundance into your day. Make FUN and ABUNDANCE your truth! After all, life is meant to be enjoyable! Maybe you share a joke with a friend, maybe you try something new and fun that you've been putting off, maybe you crank the volume on your stereo and dance around your house. Whatever you choose, just make sure you are having FUN and loving every second of it!

—◦ Empowered to A.C.T.: ◦—

What inspired **ACTION** will you take today?
What purposeful **CHANGE** will you make today?
What can you **TEACH** someone else today?

Happy Fun and Abundance!

Remember, nothing happens until you decide to take action!

Peel Back the Layers

"Life is like an onion. You peel off one layer at a time
and sometimes you weep."
~ Unknown

You have so much to experience, learn, and grow from during your lifetime. It would be silly to think all your growth takes place at one time. You experience and learn many things from various life experiences. Some are exciting and some are painful, some make you laugh and some make you cry. As you live through these experiences, it is as if you are peeling back the layer of an onion each time. You see, as you peel back the layers, you learn more and more about who you really are at your core, in your soul. Look at each of your life experiences as an opportunity to peel back a layer to reveal more of your true self!

Empowered to A.C.T.:

What inspired **ACTION** will you take today?
What purposeful **CHANGE** will you make today?
What can you **TEACH** someone else today?

Happy Peeling Back the Layers!

Remember, nothing happens until you decide to take action!

Viva the Present!

"The past blocks the flow of life into the present. The past is dead.
There is no life there, even when you dwell on a happy past.
Your body wants to be alive here and now.
To give it that gift, bring your awareness to the here and now."
~ Unknown

Unless you are learning and growing from your past, there's no sense in rehashing the past. It's the part of life you cannot change no matter what. It is what it is and there is no going back. Your past, however, can be one of your greatest teachers if you decide to be present and implement your lessons learned in the here and now. If you think about it, we are gifted with new moments to implement! Since you cannot go back and change the past, why not come alive in the here and now and devour every precious moment! Take a good look and see what you are doing with those precious and priceless moments. The here and now is waiting for you to LIVE IT UP!

⌐ Empowered to A.C.T.: ⌐

What inspired **ACTION** will you take today?
What purposeful **CHANGE** will you make today?
What can you **TEACH** someone else today?

Happy Living Up the Moment!

Remember, nothing happens until you decide to take action!

Build Lasting Relationships

"You can't build a relationship with everybody in the room
when you don't care about anybody in the room."
~ John C. Maxwell

When you meet someone at a networking event or even just out and about, do you have a desire to genuinely be curious and get to know the person? Do you care about building a genuine relationship? Most people think that sounds great and would be wonderful, however, they don't operate that way when they are out. Why not? People easily get caught up in their own business/career and put the focus on themselves and their own needs and wants of making the next sale.
If that's the case for you, then you miss out on being authentic in building a genuine relationship. Go into today as a better active listener. Be more genuinely interestED than interestING! Listen for what their values are, what is important to them, and what their greatest goals are. Don't miss out on the chance to really get to know someone and create a lasting relationship!

⌐ Empowered to A.C.T.: ¬

What inspired **ACTION** will you take today?
What purposeful **CHANGE** will you make today?
What can you **TEACH** someone else today?

Happy Building Lasting Relationships!

Remember, nothing happens until you decide to take action!

Appreciation is Where It's At!

"The aim in life is appreciation; there is no sense in not appreciating things; and there is no sense in having more of them if you have less appreciation of them."
~ Gilbert K. Chesterton

I don't know about you, but when I'm in a state of appreciation and gratitude, my soul feels full ... so full, it feels like it's spilling over. Many times I am brought to tears by all the tangible and intangible things in my life that I feel blessed to have and experience. It was years ago that Michael Beckwith taught me that it's only when you are truly grateful and appreciative for what you have, more will come into your life to be grateful and appreciative for. There's no sense in having more if you aren't grateful and appreciative for what you already have. Life is just empty otherwise. Eww, that's boring and no fun! What a waste! Be sure to spend some time expressing gratitude and appreciation today and watch how more and more great stuff comes into your life!

— Empowered to A.C.T.: —

What inspired **ACTION** will you take today?
What purposeful **CHANGE** will you make today?
What can you **TEACH** someone else today?

Happy Full Souls ... So Full They're Spilling Over!

Remember, nothing happens until you decide to take action!

What Does Your Soul Seek to Give?

"The ego is constantly concerned with trying to get what it believes it doesn't have, while the soul seeks to give everything it needs, thereby realizing that those things were already present within."
~ James Twyman

What is your soul seeking to give? How can you sense it in yourself first? I asked myself this question and noticed this past weekend when I was at my sister's house for a cookout that it brought me great joy to add more joy to them and their day. I absolutely LOVED spending time with my family and putting big smiles on my nephews' and nieces' faces! The great awareness for me was that I understood that I was only able to share that joy and happiness with them because it was already present within me! I wouldn't have been able to share what I didn't already have to share. What will you share with others today that is already present within your soul?

—⚬ Empowered to A.C.T.: ⚬—

What inspired **ACTION** will you take today?
What purposeful **CHANGE** will you make today?
What can you **TEACH** someone else today?

Happy Sharing The Gifts of Your Soul!

Remember, nothing happens until you decide to take action!

163

June

Take Responsibility

"Man is made or unmade by himself."
~ James Allen

Every morning when you wake up you get to decide who you are going to be. It is all a choice you make up in your mind. It is time everyone on this planet agrees to take full responsibility for their thinking, their emotions, their being, their actions, and their results. Some days it is easier than others, but I always do my best to choose to take full responsibility for what I am thinking, my emotional state, who I am being, what I am doing, and for what I have created—the good, the bad, and the ugly. There's rarely a day that goes by that I don't feed my mind, body, and soul with something that nurtures and fuels it to be stronger and better. What are you not taking responsibility for creating in your life that you should be? No more excuses! It is entirely up to YOU!

— Empowered to A.C.T.: —

What inspired **ACTION** will you take today?
What purposeful **CHANGE** will you make today?
What can you **TEACH** someone else today?

Happy Taking Responsibility to Create a Better You, Inside and Out!

Remember, nothing happens until you decide to take action!

Today's Featured Reader:
Tina Balaka, Greenfield, Wisconsin
"What I love about this quote is the honest truth of it. When I find myself going down the "complaining road" I stop and take a moment to ask myself, "what can I do differently to get a different result?" Sometimes it's a quick couple minutes to regroup and refocus and other times it takes more time to really sit and think about what actions need to be made to get back on the track I want to be on. Thank you for the words of wisdom, Melissa!"

What is Your Purpose?

"Identifying, acknowledging, and honoring your purpose is perhaps the most important action successful people take."
~ Jack Canfield

This is something I believe so strongly in and have such a passion for. I believe it's critical to your success and happiness in life. I love love love working with people to help them discover their purpose in life! It's something that many people never take the time to really sit down and identify, acknowledge, and honor. However, when we do take the time to do so, it can be such a profound and awakening process! It will change your life! It's not something you can do in 15 minutes or anything, but if you are committed to the process, in due time you will have a greater sense of clarity on your life's purpose and it will change your life forever! Have you identified your purpose? If not, when will you?

— Empowered to A.C.T.: —

What inspired **ACTION** will you take today?
What purposeful **CHANGE** will you make today?
What can you **TEACH** someone else today?

Happy Living a Purpose Driven Life!

Remember, nothing happens until you decide to take action!

Today's Featured Reader:
Barry Smith, Corbett, Oregon
"Discovering my purpose is something that really took me almost 46 years to do. It wasn't until I got out of my own way and took a look in the mirror, that I realized my identity was based on what I did and not who I was. Then I surrounded myself with people that understood the concept of purpose and they empowered me to find mine! Thanks for the insight, Melissa!"

YOU Are a Great Success Story Waiting To Happen!

"Every great story on the planet happened when someone decided not to give up,
but kept going no matter what."
~ Spryte Loriano

You are a great story waiting to happen, I LOVE that! Take a good look at a goal or
dream you have. Imagine what the story would sound like if you didn't give up on
it, but rather you saw it through. How would the story go? How would you describe
the persistence and commitment you had to accomplish it? How would you describe
your journey? Paint a crystal clear picture for yourself and don't leave out any
details! Now HOLD onto that vision of success! And begin to take action with your
newfound vision and inspiration! Your greatest success story is awaiting you!

⌒ Empowered to A.C.T.: ⌒

What inspired **ACTION** will you take today?
What purposeful **CHANGE** will you make today?
What can you **TEACH** someone else today?

Happy Being a Great Success Story!

Remember, nothing happens until you decide to take action!

Self-Growth Is a Must

"Very often a change of self is needed more than a change of scene."
~ Christopher Benson

Have you ever thought the grass was greener on the other side? I know I have and I've even gone over there to check it out! More often than not, the grass is NOT greener on the other side. It's usually the same ole grass, just on a different piece of land. You see, many times we are looking for happiness and brighter days in something OUTSIDE of us. We think if we just change jobs, locations, spouses even, that we'll finally be happy. We think THEY are the problem and THEY need to change! When really, WE are the ones that need to grow and change! Take a good look at your current circumstances and look for ways that YOU can embrace your own growth and change. Look for ways that you can BE more!

Empowered to A.C.T.:

What inspired **ACTION** will you take today?
What purposeful **CHANGE** will you make today?
What can you **TEACH** someone else today?

Happy Embracing Internal Self-Change!

Remember, nothing happens until you decide to take action!

JUNE 5TH

Raise Your Self-Awareness!

"Every man is free to rise as far as he's able or willing, but the degree to which he THINKS determines the degree to which he'll rise."
~ Ayn Rand

If the degree to which someone will rise depends on their level of thinking, then what is one's level of thinking dependent upon? It's their level of self-awareness! You see, if you lack the self-awareness of who you really are and what you are really capable of, you'll never think higher and greater of yourself and your possibilities. You'll get caught thinking small and less than yourself and you'll always settle in life. Raise your level of self-awareness to see who you really are in your heart and soul! See the true gifts and talents you have been given! As you do, your thinking will expand and you will find yourself rising above!

⌒ Empowered to A.C.T.: ⌒

What inspired **ACTION** will you take today?
What purposeful **CHANGE** will you make today?
What can you **TEACH** someone else today?

Happy Raising Your Level of Self-Awareness!

Remember, nothing happens until you decide to take action!

Do It Afraid!

"Inaction breeds doubt and fear. Action breeds confidence and courage. If you want to conquer fear, do not sit home and think about it. Go out and get busy."
~ Dale Carnegie

One of the many great things that my longtime mentor and friend, Paul Martinelli, has taught me is to "Do It Afraid!" It's important that we wrap our minds around the idea of taking action, even when we are afraid and uncomfortable. If we sit around and wait for the day when we have no fear, we'll be waiting for a very very very long time! Instead, choose to see the great beauty in ACTION. It ignites that part of you that knows you can indeed do it! It highlights the part of you that is capable, resourced, and ALIVE! The next time you are afraid to do something, what will you think about and do so that you can get yourself to take action?

Empowered to A.C.T.:

What inspired **ACTION** will you take today?
What purposeful **CHANGE** will you make today?
What can you **TEACH** someone else today?

Happy Taking Action Afraid!

Remember, nothing happens until you decide to take action!

What You Should Never Say!

"Never say never!"
~ Justin Bieber

OK, OK I'll admit it, I watched the Justin Bieber documentary called *Never Say Never*. I'm not a raging fan or anything, yet I do believe he's an extremely talented and gifted kid who is sharing and expressing this gift and talent with the world and I love love love that! It was interesting to hear his story and learn about how even Justin Bieber and his out-of-this-world voice got turned down for a recording contract time after time again. He was rejected for being "too young" and was told to go talk to Disney. He and "his people" didn't give up. They kept knocking on doors, going on radio show after radio show across the country until he was noticed and eventually signed a recording contract with Island Records. No matter how big of a star you are, you are going to be told NO and it is up to you to keep forging forward and never giving up and never giving into someone else's lack of belief in you!

─◌ Empowered to A.C.T.: ◌─

What inspired **ACTION** will you take today?
What purposeful **CHANGE** will you make today?
What can you **TEACH** someone else today?

Happy Always Forging Forward with Your Dream!

Remember, nothing happens until you decide to take action!

The Law of the Mirror

"The Law of the Mirror: If you see value in yourself,
then you will want to add more value to yourself."
~ John C. Maxwell

It isn't until we see the value and significance in our authentic selves that we will begin to pour time and energy into ourselves. When we see our own value we believe we can make a greater impact and that we have a purpose for being here. We are drawn to express and create greatness that we know will serve many. You will find you have a greater hunger to be, do, and have more in your life when you embrace who you really are. And for that to become your reality, you must GROW! Look in the mirror today and affirm the greatness that is flowing to, with, and through you! No, it's not conceited, but rather celebratory! Acknowledge, affirm and celebrate your value and greatness!

— Empowered to A.C.T.: —

What inspired **ACTION** will you take today?
What purposeful **CHANGE** will you make today?
What can you **TEACH** someone else today?

Happy Seeing Your True Value and Adding Even More!

Remember, nothing happens until you decide to take action!

Access Your Pure Potential

"Through silence, through meditation, and through non-judgment
you access pure potentiality."
~ Deepak Chopra

When you still your mind, you free yourself up from the non-stop thoughts that
are just chitter-chatter blocking you from accessing your pure potential. Deepak
talks about what pure potentiality is in his book, *The Seven Spiritual Laws of Success*.
He says when you access pure potentiality that you access all possibilities, infinite
creativity, pure knowledge, pure joy, freedom, and bliss! But the only way to access
all those wonderful qualities is through silence, meditation, and non-judgment.
Think about how true that really is … When we don't take the time to clear out
our thoughts and minds, we get stuck in our heads, stressed out, and overwhelmed
and that's when we block out our potential. Take some time today to still your
mind. Clear you head. Be open. Your potential is awaiting you!

⤙ Empowered to A.C.T.: ⤚

What inspired **ACTION** will you take today?
What purposeful **CHANGE** will you make today?
What can you **TEACH** someone else today?

Happy Accessing Your Pure Potential!

Remember, nothing happens until you decide to take action!

Have you Stubbed Your Toe Lately?

"You will never stub your toe standing still. The faster you go, the more chance there is of stubbing your toe, but the more chance you have of getting somewhere."
~ Charles F. Kettering

Many people like to "play it safe" and not do anything risky where they could potentially get hurt and experience pain. These people are afraid to make a bet on themselves! There's too much fear and uncertainty, so they stay stuck in their nice and cozy comfort zone. Sure, they reduce their chances of getting hurt, but the downside is that they rob themselves of experiencing something they really desire in life. I don't know about you, but I believe there is more pain STAYING STUCK and inside my comfort zone than there is when I stub my toe living life outside of my comfort zone! I encourage you today to see how stubbing your toe while living your life is just a sign that you are going places! The alternative is going nowhere!

--- Empowered to A.C.T.: ---

What inspired **ACTION** will you take today?
What purposeful **CHANGE** will you make today?
What can you **TEACH** someone else today?

Happy Stubbing Your Toe In Pursuit of Your Desires!

Remember, nothing happens until you decide to take action!

Life is Wonderful!

"What a wonderful life I've had! I only wish I had realized it sooner."
~ Sidonie Gabrielle Colette

You are blessed. Do you see it? It's important for us to take the time to realize just how gifted and blessed we really are! Now, it's important to look beyond the physical gifts in your life. Gifts and blessings go far beyond a beautiful home, a great car, and a great job. This is about seeing how wonderful your life is by the relationships you have created, the love in your heart that you express and as well as the love you receive, the breath that fills your lungs, the smile that lights up the room and on and on and on. Look beyond the surface to see how even MORE wonderful your life really is!

— Empowered to A.C.T.: —

What inspired **ACTION** will you take today?
What purposeful **CHANGE** will you make today?
What can you **TEACH** someone else today?

Happy Wonderful Life!

Remember, nothing happens until you decide to take action!

JUNE 12TH

Let's Feed the Hungry

"There is more hunger for love and appreciation
in this world than for bread."
~ Mother Teresa

Each and every one of us has a basic human need to feel love and to feel significant.
Just like we have a need for food and water, we also have a need to feel love and
connection from others and also to feel appreciated and significant enough to know
we matter in this world. Without getting these needs met, there is a void and a
deep starvation. There are so many people out there who are aching from the void
and longing for more. How can you "feed" someone today by sharing some of
your love and appreciation for them? How can you make them feel significant and
valued? Let's go out and "feed" the hungry hearts and souls out there. YOU CAN
MAKE A DIFFERENCE in someone's life today. You know that, right?!

⁓ Empowered to A.C.T.: ⁓

What inspired **ACTION** will you take today?
What purposeful **CHANGE** will you make today?
What can you **TEACH** someone else today?

Happy "Feeding" the Hungry!

Remember, nothing happens until you decide to take action!

Are You Floating Yet?

"If my thoughts are negative, I can drown in a sea of my own negativity. If my thoughts are positive, I can float on the ocean of life."
~ Louise L. Hay

Your thoughts create your experiences. Are you drowning or floating? The beautiful thing is that you have the power to choose your thoughts! So why not always choose wonderful, amazing, and empowering thoughts and always float on the ocean of life? Some will say that it's not easy to think positive all the time ... I beg to differ. It simply comes down to where you are choosing to consciously place your awareness and focus. Instead of focusing on lack, fear, and drama, why not make a shift and consciously choose to focus on all the infinite abundance, beauty, and love that surrounds you in every waking moment? It's here ... It's there ... It's EVERYWHERE! You just have to choose to see it and you'll be floating on the ocean of life!

Empowered to A.C.T.:

What inspired **ACTION** will you take today?
What purposeful **CHANGE** will you make today?
What can you **TEACH** someone else today?

Happy Floating!

Remember, nothing happens until you decide to take action!

Live More LIFE!

"Just living isn't enough," said the butterfly,
"One must also have freedom, sunshine, and a little flower."
~ Hans Christian Anderson

Going through the motions of life is never quite as fulfilling as when you are intentional and purposeful with what you are creating and experiencing. Unfortunately, so many people are like the "walking dead" in their own lives. They die well before their actual death. Don't be that kind of person! Be intentional and purposeful with your life. Don't let another moment go by that isn't full of great purpose and joy! Even the little things can make a huge difference in your life. Let the warm sunshine kiss your face, give thanks for your priceless freedom, and take a moment to stop and smell some flowers today.

⟶ Empowered to A.C.T.: ⟵

What inspired **ACTION** will you take today?
What purposeful **CHANGE** will you make today?
What can you **TEACH** someone else today?

Happy Living MORE LIFE!

Remember, nothing happens until you decide to take action!

Step FORWARD into Your Growth

"You will either step forward into growth,
or you will step backward into safety."
~ Abraham Maslow

For some, stepping forward into growth can be a very scary thing. When you're stepping forward a lot of times it means that you are breaking through a comfort zone and doing something new or different. That means you are leaving behind something that feels "familiar" and "safe" to you. The key to growth is to recognize that what's ahead serves you so much more than your current state. Shift your perception from seeing growth as something that's scary to something that's so much greater and purposeful than your current state of living and being.

⸺ Empowered to A.C.T.: ⸺

What inspired **ACTION** will you take today?
What purposeful **CHANGE** will you make today?
What can you **TEACH** someone else today?

Happy Stepping Forward into Your Growth!

Remember, nothing happens until you decide to take action!

What Do Your Experiences Tell You?

"We are where we should be, doing what we should be doing, otherwise we would be somewhere else doing something else."
~ Richard Stine

You are perfectly where you are supposed to be in life. Take a look around, observe what you are experiencing right now and ask yourself, "What does this experience say about who I am being?" Your results leave you clues. If you want to change your results and be somewhere else doing something else, then there needs to be a shift in YOU, from the inside out. There needs to be an "awakening" of who you really are who you want to be. Self-awareness is always the first step and then it's time to make some new choices to achieve those new results you want. Take 20 minutes today to reflect and observe your current experiences and results. What are they trying to tell you? What's the greater message for you? Where do you need to step up and make some new choices?

─◦ Empowered to A.C.T.: ◦─

What inspired **ACTION** will you take today?
What purposeful **CHANGE** will you make today?
What can you **TEACH** someone else today?

Happy New Self-Awareness!

Remember, nothing happens until you decide to take action

You Add Tremendous Value to Others

"Give what you have to somebody, it may be better than you think."
~ Henry Wadsworth Longfellow

Many times we underestimate just how much of a significant impact we can make in someone's life. We can forget how much value we add into someone's life just by giving what we have to give. I've thought to myself at times, "Nahhh, lil' ole me isn't making a difference." Then I have to remind myself of all the times my wonderful clients, friends, and family have reminded me of what I have added into their life. Years ago I decided to start a "Gratitude Board" in my office. It's a board that is covered in Thank You letters, Gratitude cards, and testimonials from my clients and friends. Now if I ever question my ability to add value and make an impact in others' lives, I just look up at my Gratitude Board and get the confirmation I need to know the truth. I am grateful to have had the opportunity to serve and add value to so many others worldwide! You also add tremendous value to others. What can you do to remind yourself of how you add value to others and the great impact you make on them?

⟶ Empowered to A.C.T.: ⟵

What inspired **ACTION** will you take today?
What purposeful **CHANGE** will you make today?
What can you **TEACH** someone else today?

Happy Adding Tremendous Value to Others!

Remember, nothing happens until you decide to take action!

Consistently Move Toward Your Goals

"It doesn't matter how talented you are. It doesn't matter how many opportunities you receive. If you want to grow, consistency is key."
~ John C. Maxwell

If you want to be the best of the best that you can be, whether it be the best parent you can be, the best friend, the best professional, or the best athlete you can be, it will require your consistent commitment to your growth and development. And honestly, even if being your "best you" isn't your goal and you just want to be "better" than who you are being now, it still is going to require you making a consistent commitment. If you only had to do things once to master them, we would all be masters at our craft and the journey would be over. Rather, look at it as a journey and something that requires your consistent attention, commitment, and love every day. What will you do today and consistently in the days to come that will move you toward your goal?

— Empowered to A.C.T.: —

What inspired **ACTION** will you take today?
What purposeful **CHANGE** will you make today?
What can you **TEACH** someone else today?

Happy Consistently Moving Toward Your Goals!

Remember, nothing happens until you decide to take action!

Giving Up is Not an Option!

"The opposite of trying is dying."
~ Brian Vaszily

When you stop trying, you settle and you stop LIVING! You rob yourself the gift of life when you stop trying. There's a part of each and every one of us that seeks to reach, stretch, and grow. There's a part of us that longs to leave our mark and to make a difference in the world. When you stop trying, it's like you are dead inside and that's no way to LIVE; it's actually NOT true living! I don't believe in settling, I don't believe in giving up and nor should you! It's just not an option! You have waaaay too much to offer this world and when any one of us gives up and stops trying, we all miss out! Instead, seek to keep giving life all you got ... because in a way, IT IS all you got!

⌒ Empowered to A.C.T.: ⌒

What inspired **ACTION** will you take today?
What purposeful **CHANGE** will you make today?
What can you **TEACH** someone else today?

Happy Giving Life Your ALL!

Remember, nothing happens until you decide to take action!

Shed the Excess

"To be simple is to be great."
~ Ralph Waldo Emerson

We have an excess of drama, junk and stuff in this world and we seem to be addicted to consuming even more. As a society, we seem to create more drama, collect more stuff, and eat more junk! I can't help but picture an overflowing cup in my mind. I believe those who have truly mastered life have learned how to live life more simply, or in other words, they have LET GO and detached themselves of the need of more drama, junk, and stuff both physically and emotionally. They don't identify themselves by material goods, but rather they identify with what they have within, with their true selves. Choose to let go of the excess in your life!

—⟶ Empowered to A.C.T.: ⟵—

What inspired **ACTION** will you take today?
What purposeful **CHANGE** will you make today?
What can you **TEACH** someone else today?

Happy Living Life More Simply!

Remember, nothing happens until you decide to take action!

Live Life Full On!

"Twenty years from now you will be more disappointed by the things you didn't do than by the ones you did do. So throw off the bowlines, sail away from the safe harbor. Catch the trade winds in your sails. Explore. Dream. Discover."
~ Mark Twain

What are you keeping score of, your WINS or your Coulda, Woulda, Shouldas? When you look back, do you celebrate and marvel in your amazing accomplishments or do you look back in disappointment and think, "What if I would have started this back when I first thought of it?" or "What if I would have tried XYZ?" or "I should have given it all I have." Start living full on right here, right now! Live with no regrets and without any Coulda, Woulda, Shouldas! Don't look back and wish you would have given it your all. Now is the time. The power is in the present moment. LIFE is calling you ... Come sail away!

—◦ Empowered to A.C.T.: ◦—

What inspired **ACTION** will you take today?
What purposeful **CHANGE** will you make today?
What can you **TEACH** someone else today?

Happy Living Life Full On!

Remember, nothing happens until you decide to take action!

Today's Featured Reader:
Valerie Dusing, Milwaukee, Wisconsin
"I love this message—too often we are our greatest roadblock and are focused on the rear view mirror. Not that I want to go through life with blinders on, I acquire knowledge from each 'misstep' perhaps then choose to go through, around or over the pot hole. Your messages are part of my daily routine, in fact they are part of my devotional time. Thank you, Melissa!"

Make Your Dreams Come True!

"Your dreams will come true, but you have to make them come true."
~ Michael Jackson

Dreams really do come true, my friend, but not by accident! Do you believe in your dream enough to go out there and make it your reality? I fully believe that your dreams can become your reality if, and only if, you are willing to go out there and BE and DO what it takes to be in harmony with it! Remember, your dream won't come true by accident, but rather it's knowing and believing in your dream, holding onto that vision, and taking massive action in its direction. Start today by taking one step at a time. Keep fueling your desires and keep putting one foot in front of the other until your dreams have become your reality.

— Empowered to A.C.T.: —

What inspired **ACTION** will you take today?
What purposeful **CHANGE** will you make today?
What can you **TEACH** someone else today?

Happy Making Your Dreams Come True!

Remember, nothing happens until you decide to take action!

There's ALWAYS Something to Be Grateful For!

When you rise in the morning, give thanks for the light, for your life, for your strength. Give thanks for your food and for the joy of living. If you see no reason to give thanks, the fault lies in yourself.

~ Tecumseh

There's always always always something to be grateful for, no matter what. I know at times it may seem difficult to find things to be grateful when your outside circumstances are less than ideal. But I'm here to remind you that that's just an excuse. If you look for good in your life and in the world you WILL find it, guaranteed! Every time I just simply look outside and up in the sky I feel gratitude. If I see a bird fly by or hear kids playing I feel gratitude. I even feel gratitude when I'm experiencing pain because it's a reminder that I'm still ALIVE! Look for all to be grateful for today! There's so much there, you just have to look for it!

— Empowered to A.C.T.: —

What inspired **ACTION** will you take today?
What purposeful **CHANGE** will you make today?
What can you **TEACH** someone else today?

Happy Finding an Endless List of Reasons to Be Grateful!

Remember, nothing happens until you decide to take action!

Create Your Life From Love and Peace

"There will be: No peace without love; No love without understanding; No understanding without knowledge; No knowledge without work; No work without peace."
~ Unknown

It all comes down to peace and love, folks! If you think about all the amazing and wonderful things that you have created in your life, they most likely came about from peace and love. Think about it … you can't create something loving from anger, fear, and judgment. That would be like trying to create fire from an ice cube—not gonna happen! Find the love and peace in your heart and you will have the energy and drive to seek out the knowledge you need to go further; you will look for ways to be more understanding, and you will put forth the effort to make it a reality.

⚶ Empowered to A.C.T.: ⚶

What inspired **ACTION** will you take today?
What purposeful **CHANGE** will you make today?
What can you **TEACH** someone else today?

Happy Creating Your Life From Peace and Love!

Remember, nothing happens until you decide to take action!

Feed Your Mind, Heart and Soul BEFORE It's Hungry!

"In the same way that it is a good idea to drink when you feel the indication of thirst—and therefore maintain your well-being long before dehydration is experienced—it is equally important to change the thought and release resistance at the first indication of negative emotion. When you learn to release resistance in the early, subtle stages, you must thrive."
~ Esther Hicks (Teachings of Abraham)

There is no need to wait until you are sidetracked, overwhelmed, and frustrated before you start shifting your thought process to a more positive and uplifting one. Why not choose to fill your heart and soul long before it needs it? I encourage you to incorporate a daily practice where you fill yourself up in a positive way on a regular and consistent basis. What I like to do every day is read and/or listen to an uplifting CD, meditate, and journal every evening before I go to bed. It may seem like a lot to do, but believe me, my mind, heart and soul thank me for it every day and night. How will you feed your mind, heart and soul before they get hungry?

⌐ Empowered to A.C.T.: ⌐

What inspired **ACTION** will you take today?
What purposeful **CHANGE** will you make today?
What can you **TEACH** someone else today?

Happy Happy Heart and Soul!

Remember, nothing happens until you decide to take action!

Are You Living Your Purpose?

"Knowing your purpose can dramatically enhance your experience in life. Purpose-driven people experience more fulfillment, more success, and often greater rewards than other people. Paradoxically, people who set out to live their purpose often make more money than people who set out to make money."
~ Timothy Kelly

Wow! What a quote! Have you been living purposefully? Do you seek to find great meaning and fulfillment with everything you do? Once you decide to live a purpose-driven life you will find great purpose in everything you do from the moment you wake up until the moment you go to bed. It's an amazingly fulfilling way to live! Honestly, I cannot even put into words the fulfillment, energy, and passion that comes from living a purpose-driven life! When you are motivated by passion and purpose rather than fear and pain, you become unstoppable and you create out-of-this-world results!

—⸙ Empowered to A.C.T.: ⸙—

What inspired **ACTION** will you take today?
What purposeful **CHANGE** will you make today?
What can you **TEACH** someone else today?

Happy Finding Your Truth!

Remember, nothing happens until you decide to take action!

It's Up to YOU!

"Your future depends on many things, but mostly on you."
~ Frank Tyger

You create your future ... no one else. If you decide to put your future in the hands of others, that is your choice and your doing. There is no need for the blame game here, it's simple and straightforward: you are responsible for your future! The results you get are of your own doing. I find that to be music to my ears! I love knowing that my future is in my hands and that I don't need to wait on or depend on anyone else to create something amazing in my life. I can create something amazing right here and now! This is the honor and privilege of life! So decide today to live your life by design rather than by default!

Empowered to A.C.T.:

What inspired **ACTION** will you take today?
What purposeful **CHANGE** will you make today?
What can you **TEACH** someone else today?

Happy Creating Your Future!

Remember, nothing happens until you decide to take action!

Be Your Best You!

"Whatever you are, be a good one."
~ Abraham Lincoln

I've become extremely passionate about people showing up their best selves and really putting their best foot forward! This is all you really can ask of yourself, because as long as you are giving it your best, that's all that matters. I encourage you to show up ready to get in the game of life and give it your all! I also encourage you to continually work to become better and better at what you do so you can add even more value and provide an even greater service. This is not exclusive to just your career, but consider how you show up at home, in your relationships, your self-care, etc. Consistently show up your best self in every area of your life.

— Empowered to A.C.T.: —

What inspired **ACTION** will you take today?
What purposeful **CHANGE** will you make today?
What can you **TEACH** someone else today?

Happy Being Your Best You!

Remember, nothing happens until you decide to take action!

Is the World Going Blind?

"An eye for an eye only ends up making the whole world blind."
~ Mahatma Gandhi

Why does everything have to be an equal, 50-50 trade? I scratch your back, you scratch my back. What happened to wanting to give and serve because you cared and had compassion for another human being, without expecting something in return? There are a lot of people out there who you can probably help and serve better than they can help and serve you. In those cases, does it stop you from serving them? If it does, then you're just keeping score and being a creditor. How about you throw the score sheet away and you look to serve those who need you the most by expressing your gifts and talents. The world will thank you for it … and I will too!

Empowered to A.C.T.:

What inspired **ACTION** will you take today?
What purposeful **CHANGE** will you make today?
What can you **TEACH** someone else today?

Happy Serving One Another!

Remember, nothing happens until you decide to take action!

Take One Step at a Time

"It's a cinch by the inch and hard by the yard."
~ Sally McGhee

I love setting large goals for myself! Especially the ones that make me reach, stretch, and grow. However, as much as these goals excite me, they can also scare me and overwhelm me at times. I've noticed when I get scared and overwhelmed is when I'm looking at the bigger picture and get caught up in the "how." I can't always see how I'm going to get from here to there. When I find myself in that fearful and overwhelming place, it's a great reminder to myself that I don't need to know all the steps, but rather I can surrender my need to know every little part of how my vision is going to come to fruition. I can instead focus on taking one step at a time in the right direction. I can continually assess my progress, step by step, and make adjustments along the way. As you go into your day today, look for ways to keep taking baby steps forward. Be present and focus on the task at hand. If you are scared and overwhelmed, you are focusing on the wrong thing!

Empowered to A.C.T.:

What inspired **ACTION** will you take today?
What purposeful **CHANGE** will you make today?
What can you **TEACH** someone else today?

Happy Progressing One Step at a Time!

Remember, nothing happens until you decide to take action!

July

Live Life to the Fullest

"The good thing about pain is that it means you are still alive."
~ Unknown

Don't live life dead! Don't numb yourself to life! Let's face it, living a full life brings a range of emotions and some obviously feel better than others. Pain, I'm sure, is something all of us try to avoid whenever possible. The catch, however, is that when you are trying to avoid pain, you get caught in this vicious cycle of constantly trying to protect yourself that you actually miss out on growing and living life, which actually is very painful as well. So instead of trying to avoid pain at all costs, how about live life to the fullest, with healthy caution of course, and know that when you experience pain, there is an opportunity to grow and you are experiencing LIFE! You are ALIVE! Think about what you are learning and how it can make you even stronger!

—◦ Empowered to A.C.T.: ◦—

What inspired **ACTION** will you take today?
What purposeful **CHANGE** will you make today?
What can you **TEACH** someone else today?

Happy Living Life to the Fullest!

Remember, nothing happens until you decide to take action!

Your Greatest Offering is Who You Are

"What you have most to offer others, you have to offer least of all through what you say, in greater part through what you do, but in greatest part through who you are."
~ Bob Burg

The gift is not so much in just what you say or do, but rather your projection of who you really are on the inside; inside your heart and soul. When you live an authentic and heart-centered life, you are truly sharing your greatest self with the world. Many people are disconnected from and don't even really know what is in their heart and soul. They are more in their heads than in their hearts. What is in your heart? Know your heart. See the true gift that lies within you. See the unlimited potential, greater purpose, and true value in yourself and then go live in alignment with it! The world is starving for you to share more of your greatest self!

⁓ Empowered to A.C.T.: ⁓

What inspired **ACTION** will you take today?
What purposeful **CHANGE** will you make today?
What can you **TEACH** someone else today?

Happy Sharing Your Greatest Gift ... YOU!

Remember, nothing happens until you decide to take action!

What Will You Say?

"When people are dying they say one of two things,
'I wish I had…' or 'I am glad I did….' "
~ Krish Dhanam

A few years back I got the honor of seeing Krish Dhanam speak at the Get Motivated Seminar here in Raleigh, NC. He is a great speaker and many of the things he said really resonated with me. I was reviewing my notes and I came across this quote. I know I've heard variations of this same quote before, but this time it hit me in a different way. I thought to myself there are many times I would say, "I am glad I did," but I realized I had been shining a bright light on those past accomplishments that had happened a while ago. What about the here and now? I realized in my here and now, I have many things that I want and wish to create, but haven't gone out and created them yet. This quote brought to light, yet again, the power of the present moment! Live NOW, not in the past! You can celebrate those past accomplishments and learn and grow from them, but don't shine a light too bright on them so you begin to neglect the power in the present moment to create.

⁓ Empowered to A.C.T.: ⁓

What inspired **ACTION** will you take today?
What purposeful **CHANGE** will you make today?
What can you **TEACH** someone else today?

Happy Creating New WINS Today!

Remember, nothing happens until you decide to take action!

FREEDOM!

"I am no bird; and no net ensnares me: I am a free human being
with an independent will."
~ Jane Eyre

If you feel stuck or trapped, I dare to say that you've locked yourself up in your own prison. I know that you can't always control the conditions or circumstances that surround you, but you have 100% control of how you react to them. Look at the pilgrims. They had a situation they didn't like. They wanted their own independence. They could have said, "We're stuck here, surrounded by this massive ocean with no way out," but they didn't. They got on a boat and headed across the sea. What about the 56 individuals who signed the Declaration of Independence? Some could have said they were signing their own death warrant, but they took action and chose FREEDOM. They did what most were afraid to do. They exercised their free will and went for it in a big way. I invite you to change your perspective and exercise your FREE WILL, take action, get your groove on and move forward.

— Empowered to A.C.T.: —

What inspired **ACTION** will you take today?
What purposeful **CHANGE** will you make today?
What can you **TEACH** someone else today?

Happy Being FREE!

Remember, nothing happens until you decide to take action!

Laugh Until It Hurts!

I am thankful for laughter, except when milk comes out of my nose.
~ Woody Allen

I am soooooo thankful for laughter too! Especially those big hearty barrel laughs that make your face and stomach hurt! Now, maybe it's not the prettiest if we have milk coming out of our noses, but I sure do feel good after some good hearty barrel laughs. How about you? Those of you who know me know that once I get going, I have a pretty loud laugh and others have said that it makes them start laughing too. Yes, laughing is contagious! What a great way to pass on some joy to others through laughing! Find something hilarious today, laugh out loud, and share it with your friends!

⁓ Empowered to A.C.T.: ⁓

What inspired **ACTION** will you take today?
What purposeful **CHANGE** will you make today?
What can you **TEACH** someone else today?

Happy Laughing Until Everything Hurts!

Remember, nothing happens until you decide to take action!

Serve With Joy!

"To serve is beautiful, but only if it is done with joy
and a whole heart and a free mind."
~ Pearl S. Buck

When you are serving others, your attitude matters—BIG TIME! I find myself getting really irritated by poor customer service these days. I think I'm actually a "customer service snob!" I am very aware when those serving me have a bad attitude and seem to hate life. I do my best to "cheer" them up and be a good customer, but at times it can be difficult and it can be a distraction from the experience I am trying to create. I do my best to be compassionate, yet repeat poor customer service will keep me from going back to a place. It makes me that much more appreciative of great customer service. It's such a beautiful thing and I wish it happened more often! Great service usually makes my experience better and I keep coming back for more. When you're serving others, make sure you are serving with joy and a whole heart, because it makes a BIG difference in your customers' experience.

⁘ Empowered to A.C.T.: ⁘

What inspired **ACTION** will you take today?
What purposeful **CHANGE** will you make today?
What can you **TEACH** someone else today?

Happy Serving With GREAT Joy!

Remember, nothing happens until you decide to take action!

Is the World on Your Side?

"Instead of believing the world is plotting to do you harm, choose to believe the world is plotting to do you good. Instead of seeing every difficult challenging event as a negative, see it for what it could be—something that is meant to enrich you, empower you, or advance your causes."

~ W. Clement Stone

What do you believe about the world? Do you believe the world you live in is working for you or against you? Do you see the unlimited opportunities all around you or just limitation and scarcity? Do you see the unlimited potential you have or the lack of potential and resources? You will always see in life what you are looking for. You will either see the light or the darkness. You CHOOSE! It all starts with the thoughts you choose to place your awareness and energy on. Choose to see that every single moment you experience as an opportunity to experience a more purposeful, more inspired, more empowered YOU! Even during those tough times you still make the choice to find the good, the lesson, and the opportunity from every situation. However, you will never see it if you don't start looking for it. You must choose to see it and then you will find it!

⌐ Empowered to A.C.T.: ¬

What inspired **ACTION** will you take today?
What purposeful **CHANGE** will you make today?
What can you **TEACH** someone else today?

Happy Seeing a World That Enriches and Empowers You!

Remember, nothing happens until you decide to take action!

Never Give Up Your Ideal

"Life is aspiration. Its mission is to strive after perfection, which is self-fulfillment. The ideal must not be lowered because of our weaknesses or imperfections."
~ Mahatma Gandhi

What weaknesses or imperfections do you have that you think are holding you back from realizing your life dreams and aspirations? Because of those perceived weaknesses, do you find yourself settling for less? Do you find yourself giving up too soon? Here Gandhi is beautifully encouraging you not to settle and lower your dreams simply because you currently don't feel you have the strength or skill to create your dreams, but rather, that's the journey of life. It's the journey of striving to fulfill more of your potential and to live your life's purpose to the best of your ability. Don't give up too soon! ... Actually NEVER give up! Your life's purpose is waaaaay to valuable!

⌐ Empowered to A.C.T.: ⌐

What inspired **ACTION** will you take today?
What purposeful **CHANGE** will you make today?
What can you **TEACH** someone else today?

Happy Living a Purposeful Life!

Remember, nothing happens until you decide to take action!

Manage Your "Bad" Experiences

"If you are dedicated to your growth, then you must become
committed to managing your bad experiences well."
~ John C. Maxwell

We all have our bad experiences in life. Yes, even the most successful people do
too! You know, those bad days that test your every last nerve and emotion. They're
usually less than ideal and at times the pain can feel like a punch in the heart. Now
as much as I don't care for those experiences, I know that it's part of the package
deal when we are gifted with a life. I also know that in order to keep reaching,
stretching, and growing in life, that it's important to learn from and evolve
from those bad experiences. They aren't meaningless or useless, but rather if you
take the time to process them, they become a huge component to your growth,
development and success! Be dedicated to your growth by taking the time to
process your "bad" experiences in life, because they may not be so "bad" after all!

—◦ Empowered to A.C.T.: ◦—

What inspired **ACTION** will you take today?
What purposeful **CHANGE** will you make today?
What can you **TEACH** someone else today?

Happy Managing Your "Bad" Experiences!

Remember, nothing happens until you decide to take action!

Your Beliefs Control You!

"As you begin to break all those beliefs that tell you what isn't possible, incredible things start happening to you because you don't limit yourself anymore."
~ Don Miguel Ruiz

Limiting beliefs hold you back! They get in your way of creating what your heart and soul truly longs for. Beliefs, whether they are true or false, are jam-packed with tons of power that control your every movement, act, and deed. That is the power of belief! Since your belief system has such a strong hold on you it is critically important you do the necessary inner work to make sure your beliefs are not limiting you, but rather are empowering you! It is critical to your success and happiness that you then replace the limiting beliefs with even more empowering beliefs that serve you and propel you forward in life. The power is already within you, now it's just time to get what's blocking you OUT OF YOUR WAY! This is truly why I became a coach. I love love love coaching people through their limiting blocks! If you don't have a coach, GET ONE! This is not a sales pitch. It doesn't have to be me, just get one that you work well with. It will change your life!:)

— Empowered to A.C.T.: —

What inspired **ACTION** will you take today?
What purposeful **CHANGE** will you make today?
What can you **TEACH** someone else today?

Happy Empowering Beliefs!

Remember, nothing happens until you decide to take action!

Your Response is Everything!

"Your power lies in how you respond to the circumstances which have been created in your life. Circumstances, within themselves, are inherently neutral. It is human judgment that assigns positive and negative values to those circumstances."
~ Owen Water

Your inner response to your life makes a huge difference in the life you create and experience! You see, nothing in life is good or bad, right or wrong until you judge it by relating it to something and then you label it as such. However, before you labeled it, it carried no value or weight of being positive or negative. Your power, therefore, lies in your ability to catch yourself in that moment right before you judge and label a circumstance. See that you have the power to create a whole new experience simply by seeing the situation differently. This requires your presence and awareness. See the opportunity in it rather than the setback ... see the light rather than the darkness ... see the gift rather than the loss.

—⋄ Empowered to A.C.T.: ⋄—

What inspired **ACTION** will you take today?
What purposeful **CHANGE** will you make today?
What can you **TEACH** someone else today?

Happy New Responses!

Remember, nothing happens until you decide to take action!

Break Through It!

"Life shrinks or expands in proportion to one's courage."
~ Anais Nin

We all have an unlimited amount of courage within us to face and break through our comfort zones! It's not that someone "doesn't have any" courage, but rather it's a choice of not calling it forth and exercising it. With the awareness now that WE ALL have unlimited courage (YES, that means YOU too!), how can you expand your life by calling forth and exercising more of it? Think about what mindset and energy you need to embody so you can be more courageous. What do you need to focus on? What affirmations and prayers could you say (and feel)? What exercises could you do? Journal, visualize, meditate, stand up tall, etc.? Start exercising your courage to breakthrough any limitation and watch the life you create expand to a whole new dimension!

— Empowered to A.C.T.: —

What inspired **ACTION** will you take today?
What purposeful **CHANGE** will you make today?
What can you **TEACH** someone else today?

Happy Breaking Through Your Comfort Zone!

Remember, nothing happens until you decide to take action!

Impossible? What? HUH?

"The word impossible is not in my dictionary."
~ Napoleon Bonaparte

Impossible! What? Huh? What does that mean? I, too, choose to not buy into that word. It's funny to think at a time people thought indoor hot running water was impossible, that electricity was impossible, that flying airplanes was impossible and the list goes on and on. Who is really the judge of what is possible and impossible? I am pretty sure it is NOT you and me! If you have a dream, go for it! Don't listen to the naysayers who say it's impossible! What do they really know? They are just expressing their lack of awareness and lack of faith. Choose to see and believe in the greater side of yourself and in the infinite power flowing to, with, and through you!

⎯ Empowered to A.C.T.: ⎯

What inspired **ACTION** will you take today?
What purposeful **CHANGE** will you make today?
What can you **TEACH** someone else today?

Happy Creating the Impossible!

Remember, nothing happens until you decide to take action!

Make Choices From Your Truth

"You rarely have time for anything you want in this life, so you need to make choices. And hopefully your choices can come from a deep sense of who you are."
~ Fred Rogers

There are so many wonderful things to try, experience, and master while we're here on this beautiful planet of ours. How on earth does one make a decision when there's so much to choose from? Unfortunately, many just make choices based on what's logical and comfortable to them while dismissing what their heart and gut may be telling them. How do you check in with yourself to ensure you are making the "right" decisions for yourself? Here's where knowing and being connected to your true authentic self is priceless and will serve you every time! When you know who you really are, you will naturally make choices that honor your highest and greatest good.

⌐ Empowered to A.C.T.: ⌐

What inspired **ACTION** will you take today?
What purposeful **CHANGE** will you make today?
What can you **TEACH** someone else today?

Happy Knowing Yourself!

Remember, nothing happens until you decide to take action!

The Time is Now!

"You have no guarantee of tomorrow. If you want to express love,
you had better do it now."
~ Rick Warren

What is holding you back from telling your loved ones how much you love,
appreciate, and are grateful for them? Will you feel silly or weird doing so? Do you
think they already know and therefore you don't have to tell them? Just think back
to how wonderful it is to have a loved one express their love, appreciation, and
gratitude for YOU. If feels great, doesn't it?! Even if you already know they feel
that way, it still feels wonderful to hear it again. So why not make someone else
you care about feel the same way?! There is no time like the present to express your
love, appreciation, and gratitude! What are you waiting for?

⟶ Empowered to A.C.T.: ⟵

What inspired **ACTION** will you take today?
What purposeful **CHANGE** will you make today?
What can you **TEACH** someone else today?

Happy Expressing Your Heart!

Remember, nothing happens until you decide to take action!

Refuse to Quit!

"Effort only fully releases its reward after a person refuses to quit."
~ Napoleon Hill

Having a burning desire for your highest and greatest goals is one of the best ways to ensure your commitment to see it through. After working on a goal for a period of time, many folks just end up quitting because they're not getting the result they want. I'd classify their desire as more of a hope and wish, but not an unwavering burning desire that keeps the fire inside of them alive, even in times of adversity. If you truly want to achieve your goal and refuse to quit along the way, then fuel your desire every day, multiple times a day! Read your goal card or look at your vision board and become one with your goal at least once in the morning and at night.

— Empowered to A.C.T.: —

What inspired **ACTION** will you take today?
What purposeful **CHANGE** will you make today?
What can you **TEACH** someone else today?

Happy Fueling Your Desire and Refusing to Quit!

Remember, nothing happens until you decide to take action!

Naysayers Play a Role in Your Success

"I'd like to say to all my fans out there, thanks for the support. And to all my
doubters, thank you very much because you guys have also pushed me."
~ Usain Bolt

It may sound weird, but there's a special place in my heart for all the naysayers in
my life. They don't know it, but they helped light a fire under me. It was their
doubt that led to my conviction and belief in myself. I was going to prove them
wrong! So I thank them from the bottom of my heart for the extra nudge! I also
have a very very very special place in my heart for all those who supported me
and believed I could do it! They wouldn't let me give up! I am forever grateful to
them! How about you? Who are your naysayers and who are your supporters? Take
note of how they both play a part in your success!

⁓ Empowered to A.C.T.: ⁓

What inspired **ACTION** will you take today?
What purposeful **CHANGE** will you make today?
What can you **TEACH** someone else today?

Happy Being Grateful!

Remember, nothing happens until you decide to take action!

Do You Believe in Others?

"Treat people as if they were what they ought to be,
and help them become what they are capable of being."
~ Goethe

It's important for us all to have people in our lives that believe in us.
Unfortunately, at times, we all lack the necessary belief in ourselves to go out
there and live the life we desire and we sometimes need someone else to remind
us just how powerful and capable we really are. It makes such a huge difference,
doesn't it?! I'm sure you could recall a powerful mentor, teacher, parent, or
friend whose belief in you carried you through a time where you didn't believe in
yourself. Make the commitment to pass that amazing experience onto others who
are in need of some encouragement and belief!

⌐ Empowered to A.C.T.: ⌐

What inspired **ACTION** will you take today?
What purposeful **CHANGE** will you make today?
What can you **TEACH** someone else today?

Happy Believing In Others!

Remember, nothing happens until you decide to take action!

What Are You Capable Of?

"Never be satisfied with what you achieve, because it all pales in comparison with what you are capable of doing in the future."
~ Rabbi Nochem Kaplan

Self-satisfaction can be a dangerous place to be! Why? Because when you are self-satisfied, you become complacent and stagnant. You stop reaching, stretching, and growing. Arrgghh! Don't let that happen to you! Remind yourself of the infinite power you have flowing to, with, and through you and how when you direct that power, you are capable of being and doing soooo much more than your mind thinks you can do! How will you amaze yourself today? Think about how you can BE and DO more today than you originally planned ... and then go do it!

Empowered to A.C.T.:

What inspired **ACTION** will you take today?
What purposeful **CHANGE** will you make today?
What can you **TEACH** someone else today?

Happy Being and Doing More than Your Mind Thinks!

Remember, nothing happens until you decide to take action!

Walk Your Talk

"Many people talk, not many people walk."
~ Unknown

What's the deal here? How come it seems so easy to talk a good talk, yet doesn't seem so easy to always walk that good talk? This goes back to what I believe to be the biggest gap in life, the gap between knowing and doing. We KNOW a lot, but we aren't necessarily DOING a lot! A great way to begin to close that gap is through PASSION and PURPOSE! I believe when you fall passionately in love with something of great purpose, you're willingness to take massive action sky rockets! Think of something or someone you absolutely LOVE ... Now, look at how you'll bend over backwards, you'll go the extra mile, you'll make the necessary sacrifices for that thing or that person you love. It's a big fat MUST to fall in love with your dreams, your greater purpose, and goals and then you'll be walking your talk in no time!

⌐ Empowered to A.C.T.: ⌐

What inspired **ACTION** will you take today?
What purposeful **CHANGE** will you make today?
What can you **TEACH** someone else today?

Happy Walking Your Talk!

Remember, nothing happens until you decide to take action!

Are You a Champion?

"If you want to see where someone develops into a champion,
look at their daily routine."
~ John C. Maxwell

It's your daily activity and rituals that you create that make the difference in who you become and what results you create. I remember a few years back when I was training for a full marathon. I did not really become a marathon runner on race day, but rather it was the daily commitment for the five months leading up to race day that truly made me a marathon runner. You don't achieve a big dream or become a great leader overnight. Sometimes I wish that was the case, but reality always reminds me of the process and journey to become a greater version of myself. Take a look at your own daily activities and rituals. Which ones are leading toward your goals and which ones are not?

─◌ Empowered to A.C.T.: ◌─

What inspired **ACTION** will you take today?
What purposeful **CHANGE** will you make today?
What can you **TEACH** someone else today?

Happy Becoming a Champion!

Remember, nothing happens until you decide to take action!

Be Impeccable With Your Word

"Being impeccable with your word is the correct use of your energy; it means to use your energy in the direction of truth and love for yourself."
~ Don Miguel Ruiz

First and foremost, always always always speak to yourself with kindness, truth and love and then use that energy to express yourself to others. If you use words against yourself, such as negative self-judgment, then you embody that negative energy and you use it to express yourself to others. It's toxic and serves no one! Start loving yourself by talking to yourself with kindness, love, and truth. Can you make that a priority in your life? When you create an impeccable relationship between you and you, you then are in the position to create impeccable relationships outside of yourself. The relationship between you and you always comes before outside relationships!

⸱⸱ Empowered to A.C.T.: ⸱⸱

What inspired **ACTION** will you take today?
What purposeful **CHANGE** will you make today?
What can you **TEACH** someone else today?

Happy Being Impeccable with Your INNER Word First!

Remember, nothing happens until you decide to take action!

What Are You Tolerating These Days?

"You get what you tolerate. You are constantly
teaching people how to treat you."
~ Elise Burns-Hoffman

How do you wish to be treated? Do you find people honor that? If not, realize you are setting the example. It is up to you to create boundaries that, first and foremost, YOU honor and respect. If you don't honor and respect your own boundaries, how can you expect others to? In order to create healthy boundaries for yourself, you must get very clear about what you will and won't tolerate in your life. Others speaking rudely to you, being pushed around or pushed aside, others not honoring your time being taken advantage of, being lied to, etc. It's not only important for you to know what's tolerable and what's not, but it's also important to plan ahead and know what you would do if one of your boundaries is crossed. When this happens how will you communicate? How will you handle it? What will you do/say? You see, when one of your boundaries is crossed, it will usually generate negative energy for you, so clarity and planning ahead are your friends here!

⌐ Empowered to A.C.T.: ⌐

What inspired **ACTION** will you take today?
What purposeful **CHANGE** will you make today?
What can you **TEACH** someone else today?

Happy Creating Healthy Boundaries!

Remember, nothing happens until you decide to take action!

221

Are You Due For Some Motivation?

"People often say that motivation doesn't last. Well, neither does bathing—
that's why we recommend it daily."
~ Zig Ziglar

This quote always gives me a good laugh! It makes me laugh because it's soooo
true! We can't expect our motivation to last forever without putting some effort
into it. And when I say "effort" I mean how hard is it to pop in a motivational CD
or song each morning? How hard is it to read a few paragraphs from your favorite
book each day? How hard is it to start and end your day with gratitude? How
hard it is to review your goals and vision every day? In comparison to all the other
things we have on our To Do list, getting ourselves motivated is probably one of
the easier things on the list. It's even easier than bathing daily! What can you do
right here and now in this present moment to get even more motivated?

◦⌒ Empowered to A.C.T.: ⌒◦

What inspired **ACTION** will you take today?
What purposeful **CHANGE** will you make today?
What can you **TEACH** someone else today?

Happy Daily Motivation!

Remember, nothing happens until you decide to take action!

Which Kind of Person Are You?

"There are two kinds of people in this world: those who want to get things done and those who don't want to make mistakes."
~ John C. Maxwell

Which kind of person are you? Do you wake up in the morning excited to live your life and accomplish something special each day? Or do you wake up hoping to coast through the day and escape from growing and learning something new? I believe we've probably all had both of those kinds of mornings, but you have to be honest with yourself and ask which one is more common for you. The attitude you carry into the majority of your days is going to have a huge impact on the life you experience and create for yourself. Don't let complacency and/or fear grab hold of you to the point where you stop growing and living your greatest life.

Empowered to A.C.T.:

What inspired **ACTION** will you take today?
What purposeful **CHANGE** will you make today?
What can you **TEACH** someone else today?

Happy Living Your Greatest Life!

Remember, nothing happens until you decide to take action!

Honoring Yourself Leads to Authenticity

"We need to find the courage to say no to the things and people that are not serving us if we want to rediscover ourselves and live our lives with authenticity."
~ Barbara de Angelis

Sometimes saying "no" can feel like the hardest thing to do, but I actually think saying "yes" to yourself can seem even harder. When you say "yes" to yourself you are honoring yourself. It's amazing what can happen when you do that. You see, when you actually make yourself a priority and create healthy and purposeful boundaries, you open yourself up to embracing your authenticity. Your authentic self isn't afraid to say that it has needs or that something isn't serving it. It seeks people and environments that serve your highest and greatest good. Truly being authentic with yourself and others will lead you toward creating a wonderful and beautiful life!

⸙ Empowered to A.C.T.: ⸙

What inspired **ACTION** will you take today?
What purposeful **CHANGE** will you make today?
What can you **TEACH** someone else today?

Happy Honoring Yourself!

Remember, nothing happens until you decide to take action!

Vacations ROCK!

"Vacation used to be a luxury,
but in today's world it has become a necessity."
~ Unknown

Let me confess, every time I take a vacation, I set the intention of getting some work done while I'm vacationing. I know, it's absurd and yet still, I do it every time. I bring my laptop, my books, my notes, and yes, every time, my vacation gets the best of me and I end up "shutting down" my office and soaking up every minute of relaxation and reflection. I RECHARGE my batteries and boy, oh, boy, do I feel great afterward! My mind, body and soul thank me for it too! What I have learned the long and slow way is the great importance of taking a vacation or break from "the office" and soaking up very precious moment. It's so super important to schedule breaks into your schedule so that you can let go of the day-to-day chaos that stresses you out and truly unplug and recharge! When you take time to let go of the chaos, you LET IN insights and gain a new awareness. When was your last vacation or break? Just a hunch, but I think you may be due? Schedule in your next vacation or break!

—๑ Empowered to A.C.T.: ๑—

What inspired **ACTION** will you take today?
What purposeful **CHANGE** will you make today?
What can you **TEACH** someone else today?

HAPPY VACATION!

Remember, nothing happens until you decide to take action!

Reignite Your Faith and Desire

"In order to succeed, your desire for success
should be greater than your fear of failure."
~ Bill Cosby

My business partner, mentor, and friend, John C. Maxwell, taught me years ago
not to try and eliminate fear, but rather to build my faith and desire to be stronger
than fear. Whichever is stronger WINS! If you are wishy-washy with your faith
and desire, you will not meet with success. And even if you do meet with success,
it will take all you've got to maintain and keep it! Take some time today to put
some energy into your faith and desire. Reignite them! There's great power in
them! Your success depends on it!

⸻ Empowered to A.C.T.: ⸻

What inspired **ACTION** will you take today?
What purposeful **CHANGE** will you make today?
What can you **TEACH** someone else today?

Happy Rock Solid Faith and Desire!

Remember, nothing happens until you decide to take action!

How Does One Achieve Success?

"Success is the sum of small efforts, repeated day in and day out."
~ Robert Collier

You don't achieve success in just one step. Just like you don't make it to the top of a mountain in one step, you don't build a beautiful relationship in just one step, you don't master your craft and your business in just one step. Success is something you work at every day, step by step, and day by day. It's a lifelong commitment to a way of living. You study, you practice, you execute, you perform, and you repeat. Whether it is your first step or your 1,000th step, you take the step the same way; you put one foot in front of the other. No need to overcomplicate the process.

⟶ Empowered to A.C.T.: ⟵

What inspired **ACTION** will you take today?
What purposeful **CHANGE** will you make today?
What can you **TEACH** someone else today?

Happy Steps to Success!

Remember, nothing happens until you decide to take action!

Today's Featured Reader:
Heidi Endicott, Milwaukee, Wisconsin
"Thanks, Melissa for those words. I am so excited to be taking more steps forward not only for myself, but for my family, and for my business. When I am committed, anything is possible!"

Self-Love Rocks!

"Turns out that loving yourself is the greatest way to improve yourself, and as you improve yourself, you improve your world."
~ Joe Vitale

Ahhhh … breathe that in … that's such a great quote! I find it interesting though how difficult at times it can be to love ourselves. So many people really struggle to allow themselves to be loved by thy self. People fear coming across selfish or conceited or even worse yet, some people don't feel worthy of self-love. I invite you to try out this self-love exercise: dip down into your heart space for a moment (close your eyes and take a few deep breaths and feel your awareness dip down into your heart). Find that warm place in your heart where you hold love (you may need to think of a loved one or something you love). Let that feeling swell up. Now imagine that warmth and love flowing into every inch of your body … your fingers, your hair, your smile, your toes, your elbows. Really feel your love flow EVERYWHERE! As you feel it go into the different parts of your body say, "I love my fingers, I love my toes, I love my smile …" and so on and so on. The key to this exercise is that you actually FEEL the love traveling through every part of your body! The more you do this, the more you'll find an unconditional love for every inch of your mind, body, and spirit!

⟶ Empowered to A.C.T.: ⟵

What inspired **ACTION** will you take today?
What purposeful **CHANGE** will you make today?
What can you **TEACH** someone else today?

Happy Loving Yourself!

Remember, nothing happens until you decide to take action!

Are You Hooked on Negativity?

"Often times we actually become attached to and invested in these negative feeling states, making them much more difficult, if not impossible, to overcome."
~ Katherine Woodward Thomas

Are you attached to your fear and drama? Sometimes we can get caught up in our own stories and have a hard time letting them go. We get caught up in the drama of them and actually create the habit of drama, conflict, and fear. What stories are you hanging onto that fill you with drama, conflict, and fear? These stories need to be released! Ask yourself, "What negative story am I putting waaaaaay too much time and energy into?" I'm sure there is a better use of your time and energy than rehashing some old negative story that just creates more fear and drama. It really doesn't serve you or others. Take some time to think today about how you can detach yourself from stories that create a negative feeling for you. Once and for all detach from the fear and drama and set yourself free!

⟶ Empowered to A.C.T.: ⟵

What inspired **ACTION** will you take today?
What purposeful **CHANGE** will you make today?
What can you **TEACH** someone else today?

Happy Letting Go!

Remember, nothing happens until you decide to take action!

229

August

True Happiness Means Living Purposefully!

"Many persons have a wrong idea of what constitutes true happiness. It is not attained with self-gratification but through fidelity to a worthy purpose."
~ Helen Keller

Yet another powerful quote regarding PURPOSE! I love it! Your true happiness comes from you choosing to honor and LIVE out your purpose every day! When you make the choice to honor and live your purpose, you are making a choice to allow and welcome great joy and happiness into your life. A great way to know if you living purposefully is to ask yourself if the choices you are making lift you up or drag you down … serve you or work against you … energize you or drain you? You see, living your purpose should bring you your greatest energy and fulfillment! It's in living a life of great fulfillment and energy that we find our greatest happiness!

⌒ Empowered to A.C.T.: ⌒

What inspired **ACTION** will you take today?
What purposeful **CHANGE** will you make today?
What can you **TEACH** someone else today?

Happy Living Purposefully!

Remember, nothing happens until you decide to take action!

Does Your Success Feel Good in Your Heart?

"If your success is not on your own terms, if it looks good to the world, but does not feel good in your heart, it is not success at all."
~ Anna Quindlen

The most fulfilling and rewarding successes are not the ones where the world cries, "Bravo! You did it!" but rather it's the successes where your heart cries, "Bravo! You followed your calling! That feels amazing!" Unfortunately many people work so hard for an achievement just because it's what someone else wants or it's what society tells them they should do. Once they achieve it they are still left feeling empty and unfulfilled. It's important to listen to your heart and be led to what is really calling you. Only when your heart's desires are listened to and acted upon will you truly be fulfilled in life. Do your successes feel good to your heart?

⌒ Empowered to A.C.T.: ⌒

What inspired **ACTION** will you take today?
What purposeful **CHANGE** will you make today?
What can you **TEACH** someone else today?

Happy Heart Successes!

Remember, nothing happens until you decide to take action!

Choose to Be Your Best!

"Eaters eat; runners run; guilty people feel guilty; angry people get angry;
achievers find a way; victims find a reason."
~ Anthony Robbins

Who are you BEING most of the time? You see, who you choose to be day in and
day out is creating your reality and your destiny. Take a look at your behaviors.
They will tell you who you've been being and what you've been getting. The great
beauty about this magnificent life you've been gifted with is that if you don't like
what you see, then you can change it! Why not choose to be the person you know
would honor who you are and where you want to go in life? There is nothing
stopping you from being and doing that. You get to choose! Choose to live with
purpose. Choose to be full of energy. Choose to be purposeful, energetic, and full of
life and make a real difference in the world. It's your choice.

~ Empowered to A.C.T.: ~

What inspired **ACTION** will you take today?
What purposeful **CHANGE** will you make today?
What can you **TEACH** someone else today?

Happy Choosing to Be Your Best!

Remember, nothing happens until you decide to take action!

Your Heart's Greatest Desire

"I believe there's an inner power that makes winners or losers and the winners are the ones who really listen to the truth of their hearts."
~ Sylvester Stallone

When you listen to your heart and follow its desire is when you live a life full of purpose and truth. Just remember, your heart's greatest and deepest desire is always seeking your highest and greatest good. Your heart longs for you to live a life full of truth, purpose, and joy! To go against yourself and live a life of lack and unhappiness is not honoring your greater truth and purpose; it's not honoring who you really are. I find whenever I'm not listening to my heart is when fear and doubt creep in. How about you? What do you notice? I also get easily distracted and those nasty thoughts that beat me down seem to take over. It's a trigger to let me know I need to reconnect to my heart and my truth. I'll take a few nice deep breaths and drop my awareness down into my body and into my heart space. I remind myself of who I really am and my greater truth. It recharges me!

─◌ Empowered to A.C.T.: ◌─

What inspired **ACTION** will you take today?
What purposeful **CHANGE** will you make today?
What can you **TEACH** someone else today?

Happy Connecting to Your Heart's Desire!

Remember, nothing happens until you decide to take action!

Today's Featured Reader:
Chris Lange, Laguna Hills, California
"I used this quote in my weekly sales meeting! Many more are also very good! Thanks, Melissa!"

236

Believe in Unlimited Solutions

"Prepare to let go of ALL your useless excuses for why you can't do something, and instead FIND A WAY TO DO IT."
~ Jonathan Budd

Excuses are just reasons to stay stuck and not develop a new belief that you know will serve you. Do you really think your excuses are going to go away on their own? Sorry to say, but you're not going to wake up one day and by chance all your excuses are gone. If you want new results in your life, it's up to YOU to do something about it. Empower yourself to know that you can find a solution to move forward. But first, you must expect and believe there is a way, a solution, an answer. It's there, but you won't start looking for it if you don't expect or believe to find it. Believe in unlimited solutions! You may even surprise yourself with how many solutions and options are out there!

⁓ Empowered to A.C.T.: ⁓

What inspired **ACTION** will you take today?
What purposeful **CHANGE** will you make today?
What can you **TEACH** someone else today?

Happy Believing in Unlimited Solutions!

Remember, nothing happens until you decide to take action!

237

Does Fear Own You?

"To feel fear is one thing. To let fear grab you by the tail
and swing you around is another."
~ Katherine Paterson

Everyone has fear. Yes, everyone! But not everyone lets fear own and control them. Not everyone is bullied by fear to a point where it paralyzes them from moving forward in life. Those who have developed the ability to see fear as a normal human emotion, know that the only way to not let it control and own them is to build their faith to be stronger! Don't try and eliminate fear, but rather build your faith to be stronger than your fear! The stronger of the two will "win" you over!

— Empowered to A.C.T.: —

What inspired **ACTION** will you take today?
What purposeful **CHANGE** will you make today?
What can you **TEACH** someone else today?

Happy Building Your Faith to Be Stronger Than Your Fear!

Remember, nothing happens until you decide to take action!

Evolve Your Consciousness

"Life will give you whatever experience is most helpful in the evolution of your consciousness. How will you know this is the experience you need? Because it is the experience you are having at this moment."

~ Kelly Sylte

I believe life is meant to be experienced and each experience leaves us with a greater awareness of life and who we are. We are meant to expand with life. If something has made you sad, feel sad. If something made you angry, allow yourself to be angry. Of course you don't want to marinate in those emotions, but you can allow them to pass through and release them. Give yourself permission to experience what life brings without judgment and notice the freedom and joy it brings for you as well as the evolution in your consciousness.

⟿ Empowered to A.C.T.: ⟿

What inspired **ACTION** will you take today?
What purposeful **CHANGE** will you make today?
What can you **TEACH** someone else today?

Happy Experiencing What You're Experiencing!

Remember, nothing happens until you decide to take action!

The Power is in the Present Moment

"Do not dwell in the past, do not dream of the future,
concentrate the mind on the present moment."
~ Buddha

I find when I'm coaching my clients that they experience pain when they focus on the past and frustration when they focus on the future. That's when I call them into this present moment. The only time you have a choice to do something new or different is right here right now. The power is ALWAYS in the present moment. Focus on and take note of the choices and opportunities you are presented with in this present moment—not yesterday and not tomorrow—but today, here and now.

Empowered to A.C.T.:

What inspired **ACTION** will you take today?
What purposeful **CHANGE** will you make today?
What can you **TEACH** someone else today?

Happy Focusing on the Present!

Remember, nothing happens until you decide to take action!

Are You On the Path of Personal Excellence?

*"The will to win, the desire to succeed, the urge to reach your full potential ...
these are the keys that will unlock the door to personal excellence."*
~ Confucius

Do you believe "if there's a will, there's a way?" Do you have a burning desire in your heart to succeed? Do you seek to reach, stretch, and grow? If you answered "No" to any of these questions, then your personal excellence may be in jeopardy. You may not be getting the results you want and are wondering why. If you answered "Yes" to all three of these questions, then you are on the path of personal excellence! Where are you at? Where might there be an opportunity for greater alignment with your personal excellence? More will? More desire? More reaching, stretching, and growing? Assess where you're at and make a decision to do something about it today!

⁓ Empowered to A.C.T.: ⁓

What inspired **ACTION** will you take today?
What purposeful **CHANGE** will you make today?
What can you **TEACH** someone else today?

Happy Personal Excellence!

Remember, nothing happens until you decide to take action!

Learn From the Drama, But Don't Become the Drama

"I am thankful for all those difficult people in my life, they have shown me exactly who I do not want to be."
~ Unknown

We've all at one time or another had people in our lives who are difficult, negative, and/or dramatic. At times you may ask, "Why on earth is this person in my life! Am I being punished for something?" Well, here's a new way to look at those people and situations. Be grateful they've entered your life for they come bearing huge insight and awareness for you. They are showing you more of who you choose NOT to be and what doesn't suit your highest and greatest good. As a matter of fact, next time one of those people are behaving in a way that doesn't suit you, step back and reflect. Make sure that you're not dishing that out to someone else. You can even use their behavior as a gauge of what NOT to do and do the opposite. When you change the way you see these people and begin feeling grateful that they have provided you with some valuable insight they'll magically fade away. Then the drama can be saved for the theater.

—◦ Empowered to A.C.T.: ◦—

What inspired **ACTION** will you take today?
What purposeful **CHANGE** will you make today?
What can you **TEACH** someone else today?

Happy Being Grateful for the Drama Kings and Queens!

Remember, nothing happens until you decide to take action!

Create Deeper Connections With One Another

"We must learn to live together as brothers or perish together as fools."
~ Martin Luther King

We all know that when we come together we are much stronger, creative, and more connected than when we work on our own and/or against one another. Just think of all the wonderful blessings we miss out on when we disconnect and distance ourselves from our brothers and sisters. It's quite foolish, isn't it?! Seek to reconnect with one another today, work together to find solutions, answers, and heal the wounds we all have. This requires you to connect beyond just the surface. Come together at a deeper more meaningful level. At the end of the day, it comes down to our relationships and how we treat each other. Who will you connect with today?

―⸱ Empowered to A.C.T.: ⸱―

What inspired **ACTION** will you take today?
What purposeful **CHANGE** will you make today?
What can you **TEACH** someone else today?

Happy Deeper Connections!

Remember, nothing happens until you decide to take action!

Are You an Optimist?

*"Optimism is essential to achievement and it is also the
foundation of courage and of true progress."*
~ Unknown

What do you want to create this month and/or year? Are you optimistic about it?
Your optimism is a necessity, not an option, when it comes to creating success in
your life. Without optimism, it's like you're working toward your goal in the dark.
Unless you have eyes in the back of your head and night vision, you're not going
to get too far! Now I'm not talking about just positive thinking and puppies and
sunshine. I'm talking about your attitude overall! Let's face it, with a bad attitude,
nothing's going to happen. Take a look at your goals for the month and/or year
and really feel what type of attitude you have toward it. Are you optimistic or
pessimistic? Do your goals ignite a passion and excitement or a stress and anxiety?
It's important to know what type of attitude is backing your goals. It will have a
huge impact on what type of effort you put toward achieving your goal and how
you'll ultimately feel toward it. Choose to believe in yourself and be optimistic
about what's possible for you!

⟶ Empowered to A.C.T.: ⟵

What inspired **ACTION** will you take today?
What purposeful **CHANGE** will you make today?
What can you **TEACH** someone else today?

Happy Optimism!

Remember, nothing happens until you decide to take action!

Live and Lead With Passion

"Someone with information can lead hundreds.
Someone with PASSION can lead thousands."
~ Julio Melara

Ahhh, passion! One of my fav topics! Those who lead with passion don't have to "try" to get followers; they just naturally draw in those who are in harmony with their passion and purpose. Passion inspires! Purpose gives life! Passion energizes and lifts us up! Purpose gives us a greater cause and reason for being committed to doing what we're doing! We are just naturally drawn to those who lead with their passion and purpose. If you are seeking to lead many with your message and purpose, don't seek to "get" more followers, but rather let your passion and purpose ooze (yes, "ooze" is a technical term) right out of you and those who are in harmony with your message will naturally and effortlessly be drawn to you.

Empowered to A.C.T.:

What inspired **ACTION** will you take today?
What purposeful **CHANGE** will you make today?
What can you **TEACH** someone else today?

Happy Living and Leading With Passion!

Remember, nothing happens until you decide to take action!

245

Watch a Good Leader in Action!

"Leadership is more caught than taught. How does one 'catch' leadership? By watching good leaders in action. The majority of leaders emerge because of the impact made on them by established leaders who modeled leadership and mentored them."
~ John C. Maxwell

I feel so honored and privileged because I have been led by some amazing world-class leaders and mentors and I'd like to highlight one in particular, Paul Martinelli. He truly has inspired me to want to follow his lead. He's a great example of his word and is always seeking to better himself and his team through his every movement, act, and deed. I hope that some of it has rubbed off on my own leadership! Who in your life has been a true leader and mentor to you? Take time to highlight this person. Acknowledge how their leadership has been such a great example to you and how it has positively impacted how you now lead.

─◌ Empowered to A.C.T.: ◌─

What inspired **ACTION** will you take today?
What purposeful **CHANGE** will you make today?
What can you **TEACH** someone else today?

Happy Great Leaders and Mentors in Your Life!

Remember, nothing happens until you decide to take action!

What Are Your Natural Talents?

"You become successful when you exploit your natural talents. Tom Hanks, and anyone else you can think of who is, or was, wildly successful at what they do, work to the bone at becoming even better at what they are naturally gifted at doing."
~ Michael Port

I have to say, leaving my "day job" and following my natural talents as a trainer, coach, and speaker has been the best decision of my life! It has led to my greatest successes and I have never felt so "in my skin" than I do now! What are your natural talents? What talent naturally flows out of you? The next important question to ask yourself is, have you found a way to do it for a living? We all have natural talents and there is really no reason to not strengthen them and make a living out of it. Why pass up the chance to get paid for what you love and are naturally good at? When you are doing what you love and what you are naturally good at, your best self and your best work shines through and you naturally love every minute of the day!

⌒ Empowered to A.C.T.: ⌒

What inspired **ACTION** will you take today?
What purposeful **CHANGE** will you make today?
What can you **TEACH** someone else today?

Happy Natural Talents!

Remember, nothing happens until you decide to take action!

Take Care of Yourself

"If you disregard your own health and well-being to take care of others,
you soon won't have much to offer them."
~ Chris Tolp

What a great quote! So often we forget to take care of ourselves because we are so busy taking care of others and making sure everyone else is happy. It is great to be in service to others, but in order for us to be able to be at our best and give the best gift of them all, ourselves, we can't neglect our own needs. Take time to recharge your batteries, to pamper yourself, to participate in an activity that brings you joy. All these are so important for us to be our very best so that when we care for others we get our very best selves, and not our drained, short tempered, and exhausted selves! That doesn't do anyone any good, does it?! Recharge your batteries today and fall in looooove with taking care of yourself.

⟶ Empowered to A.C.T.: ⟵

What inspired **ACTION** will you take today?
What purposeful **CHANGE** will you make today?
What can you **TEACH** someone else today?

Happy Taking Care of Yourself!

Remember, nothing happens until you decide to take action!

The Here and Now

"Real generosity toward the future lies in giving all to the present."
~ Albert Camus

Too often we get caught up in the thoughts and emotions that come from the past or from the future and it can be difficult to focus on giving the present moment all you got. What if the best thing you could do for your future was to focus on the present moment? It may seem counterintuitive, however when you give the present moment all you have to give, you basically set yourself up for success in the next moment ... and the next ... and the next. So the power is in this very moment here and now. I'm a huge advocate of preparation and planning, so when it comes to moving toward that goal, work your plan and continually put your best foot forward.

— Empowered to A.C.T.: —

What inspired **ACTION** will you take today?
What purposeful **CHANGE** will you make today?
What can you **TEACH** someone else today?

Happy Giving the Here and Now All You've Got!

Remember, nothing happens until you decide to take action!

Fear Not!

"To fear love is to fear life, and those who fear life
are already three parts dead."
~ Bertrand Russell

I believe those who fear love really just fear rejection, failure, and being hurt.
We've all been there at one point or another. If we can steer clear of it, why not,
right?! Well, the big danger is that then we end up hiding behind invisible walls
and pretending to be someone we are not just to "protect" ourselves from being
hurt we end up hiding and running from LIFE! It's through being loving, living
life, and being vulnerable that we get to be more of who we really are and live life
more fully and purposefully. We get to embrace love, and that's priceless! Sure,
it takes work, but believe me, as a student of working through my own fears, at
times it's not easy; however, the alternative is to let a part of you die, and in my
book, that's not an option.

Empowered to A.C.T.:

What inspired **ACTION** will you take today?
What purposeful **CHANGE** will you make today?
What can you **TEACH** someone else today?

Happy Living and Loving Life!

Remember, nothing happens until you decide to take action!

Learn to Live Like Nature Does

"Contemplate the flowers and learn from them how to live."
~ Jesus

Look at the flower. It doesn't worry about whether it will bloom or not, get enough sun or not, or get enough water or not. It doesn't say, "Wow, I sure hope the sun shines today." Or "That rose over there is so beautiful and fragrant and I'm just a little daisy." No, it says, "Good mooooorning, world. Look at me, so bright and ALIVE." A flower simply opens up to the light and receives all that it needs. It doesn't have to try. It doesn't have to force it. It merely allows itself to BE. Today I challenge you to allow yourself to BE YOURSELF, who you really are. When you live from your authentic self, the actions you take will be in alignment and success will follow. Allow your SOUL to blossom and show the world your true self.

Empowered to A.C.T.:

What inspired **ACTION** will you take today?
What purposeful **CHANGE** will you make today?
What can you **TEACH** someone else today?

Happy Learning and Living Like Nature Does!

Remember, nothing happens until you decide to take action!

Happiness is Awaiting You Right Now

"Happiness is not something you postpone for the future;
it is something you design for the present."
~ Jim Rohn

So often people are waiting for the future to happen so they can now be happy in their lives. They place a level of dependency on what may happen and disregard what's happening in the present. I know that circumstances are not always ideal, but honestly, that's no reason to not allow yourself to be happy here and now. Thinking that you can't be happy until you lose those 20 lbs, or until you make more money, or until you have better relationships, etc. is absurd. The only one that truly suffers is YOU! If you choose to look for happiness and joy in this present moment, you will find it. No need to wait!

⌐ Empowered to A.C.T.: ⌐

What inspired **ACTION** will you take today?
What purposeful **CHANGE** will you make today?
What can you **TEACH** someone else today?

Happy Happiness in the Present!

Remember, nothing happens until you decide to take action!

Keep Your Burning Desire for Success On Fire

*"Edison failed 10,000 times before he made the electric light.
Do not be discouraged if you fail a few times."*
~ Napoleon Hill

Why do you think Edison refused to quit even after all that failure? After studying Edison for a few years now, I can now see how he always chose to see the success and possibility in his experiments rather than failure. He would say things like, "I discovered 10,000 ways how electricity does NOT work." What an attitude! I love it! What about you? What do you say when you experience failures? How do you keep your burning desire for success on fire? It's up to YOU to keep the fire alive, regardless of the outcome!

⸺ Empowered to A.C.T.: ⸺

What inspired **ACTION** will you take today?
What purposeful **CHANGE** will you make today?
What can you **TEACH** someone else today?

Happy Keeping Your Desire On Fire!

Remember, nothing happens until you decide to take action!

Be Grateful for the "No"s

"I am thankful to all those who said no to me.
It's because of them, I did it myself."
~ Albert Einstein

Thank goodness for NO. It may feel bad at first, but if you reflect back on the many times you have probably heard that in your life, you would find many things of which to be grateful. When the "no" comes, it might hurt at first because it was contrary to your expectation or desire. But like Albert Einstein pointed out, the NO's didn't make him give up. They created a challenge to do something on his own. Now I would say that Albert Einstein definitely made his mark on the world. Don't let something as simple as a "NO" stop you from making yours. Take the "NO" and go for it. I guarantee you've got it in you!

⟶ Empowered to A.C.T.: ⟵

What inspired **ACTION** will you take today?
What purposeful **CHANGE** will you make today?
What can you **TEACH** someone else today?

Happy Thanking the "NO"s!

Remember, nothing happens until you decide to take action!

Do You Love Yourself?

"When you are strong enough to love yourself 100%, good and bad—you will be amazed at the opportunities that life presents you."
~ Stacey Charter

I call self-judgment the "death of a million paper cuts." You are killing yourself little by little with each thought of self-judgment. You cut yourself down, you beat yourself up, and before you know it, you actually begin to believe the lies and you shut the doors of opportunity! How about you cause an interruption in that rubbish and decide to think a bit higher and grander of yourself today? When you choose to acknowledge and love the gifts you have been given, life brings you opportunities to share those gifts with the world!

⌐ Empowered to A.C.T.: ⌐

What inspired **ACTION** will you take today?
What purposeful **CHANGE** will you make today?
What can you **TEACH** someone else today?

Happy Loving Yourself From Head to Toe and Inside and Out!

Remember, nothing happens until you decide to take action!

Struggles Are Your Pathway to Success

"Our struggles are the short term lessons we learn to
achieve long term success."
~ Simon Sinek

What is the real purpose of a struggle? I mean, they're not much fun and many
times they are quite annoying because they happen when you don't want them
to! But what if it were these moments that come at the worst time and seem to
be jam-packed with problems and frustrations that bring us our greatest gifts?
What if these moments are exactly what we need to achieve our greatest joys and
to transform and evolve beyond where we currently are? What if these struggles
are the pathway to our greatest successes? Look at your short term struggles as
the exact experiences that you need to go through in order to learn and grow and
achieve great success!

⟶ Empowered to A.C.T.: ⟵

What inspired **ACTION** will you take today?
What purposeful **CHANGE** will you make today?
What can you **TEACH** someone else today?

Happy Great Successes!

Remember, nothing happens until you decide to take action!

The REAL American Dream!

"The REAL American Dream is not about a garage full of new cars, winning the lottery, or retiring to a life of ease in Florida. It's about doing work that has meaning, work that makes a difference, and doing that work with people you care about."
~ Joe Tye

I had the honor of experiencing something the other day that gave me a wonderful reminder that the work I do DOES have great meaning and DOES make a difference in people's lives. I needed it that day. Do you sometimes need that reminder as well? I encourage you to re-identify the importance of the work you do. Find the evidence where you can re-affirm to yourself how many times to make a difference in others' lives. Connect with that every day! If you feel the work you do doesn't have great meaning for you or make a difference the way you would like, you are in a position of choice to now find something to add, shift, change, or remove from your life to create YOUR American Dream!

—✧ Empowered to A.C.T.: ✧—

What inspired **ACTION** will you take today?
What purposeful **CHANGE** will you make today?
What can you **TEACH** someone else today?

Happy Living the American Dream!

Remember, nothing happens until you decide to take action!

Feed Possibility!

"Live as if the possibilities you long for actually do exist."
~ Geneen Roth

Too often we lack the belief in the possibilities of that which we desire. We say, "That will never happen to me ... It would take a miracle ... I wish I could do that, but ... If only XYZ wasn't in my way ..." You see, we get caught up in telling ourselves a story which is saturated in DISBELIEF and then we FEED that story and then we wonder why it grows stronger and louder! We must cause an interruption in that story and begin to tell a new one, one that is saturated in rock solid BELIEF! You must focus on the possibility of what you desire really does exist and you really can create it for yourself. You can FEED it and I guarantee your belief in the possibility of it will grow! You will begin to see the potential of it coming true all around you! Do you believe it's really possible? If so, then FEED IT!

—⟡ Empowered to A.C.T.: ⟡—

What inspired **ACTION** will you take today?
What purposeful **CHANGE** will you make today?
What can you **TEACH** someone else today?

Happy Feeding the Possibilities!

Remember, nothing happens until you decide to take action!

Do You Trust Your Gut?

"Good instincts usually tell you what to do
long before your head has figured it out."
~ Michael Burke

Unfortunately as we grow older we are conditioned to only tune into what our head says and ignore what our gut instincts says. Now, there's nothing wrong with listening to your head, it's just when your gut instincts are telling you something different we have to believe our gut has a good reason for doing so. When there's a contrast, it is important not to ignore your gut instincts. It's also just as important to not only listen, but to trust and FOLLOW your gut instincts as well. Realize that your gut is not trying to get your attention for no reason, there is indeed a reason and it's your responsibility to listen to it, trust it, and follow it. I fully believe that my gut always has my highest and greatest good in mind. It's always looking out for me. Don't let your mind talk you out of discovering what the true message is!

⎯ Empowered to A.C.T.: ⎯

What inspired **ACTION** will you take today?
What purposeful **CHANGE** will you make today?
What can you **TEACH** someone else today?

Happy Trusting Your Gut!

Remember, nothing happens until you decide to take action!

How Do You Feel About Yourself?

"It has been my experience that the better I feel about myself,
the more effective I am in my life and work."
~ Lou Cassara

How do you feel about yourself? We all have our good days and bad days, but on average, where are you at? What seems to be the dominating thoughts you have about yourself? When you don't feel good about yourself then there is a disconnect between the Truth you know and the truth you are living. You know deep down in your heart and soul your value and greatness, but you don't always live that way. You get in our own way at times. We all do. It's important to dedicate yourself to daily rituals and practices that keep you connected to your inner Truth of who you really are and the greatness that lies within you! When you do, your entire life will reflect your improved feelings!

꜍ Empowered to A.C.T.: ꜍

What inspired **ACTION** will you take today?
What purposeful **CHANGE** will you make today?
What can you **TEACH** someone else today?

Happy Feeling Great About YOU!

Remember, nothing happens until you decide to take action!

Keep the Spark ALIVE

"At times our own light goes out and is rekindled by a spark from another person.
Each of us has cause to think with deep gratitude of those
who have lighted the flame within us."
~ Albert Schweitzer

There are so many people who have inspired, energized, and empowered me along the way! They're such a large part of my journey and the successes that I've had. They breathed belief into me the days I didn't believe in myself, they wouldn't let me give up the times I was too tired to go on, and the days I "didn't feel like it" were the days they made me get back up again. They wouldn't let the spark within me die; they rekindled it time and time again. I am beyond grateful to them! How about you? Who has helped keep your spark alive? Be sure to express your deepest gratitude toward them!

─◦ Empowered to A.C.T.: ◦─

What inspired **ACTION** will you take today?
What purposeful **CHANGE** will you make today?
What can you **TEACH** someone else today?

Happy Rekindled Spark!

Remember, nothing happens until you decide to take action!

Smile BIG Today!

"It's a great day to smile!"
~ Sandi Krakowski

Take a look around … there is so much to smile about, isn't there?! And guess what? When you smile, the world smiles back at you! Take time today to smile about your life, your loved ones, the big blue sky, your favorite song, your favorite pet, the eggs you had for breakfast today. And don't forget to smile about the non-tangible! What about the brilliant IDEA you were gifted with in the shower this morning, or the WARMTH IN YOUR HEART when you saw a cute baby commercial, or that funny video that made your stomach hurt because you LAUGHED SO HARD, or how about the FAITH you have in your goal coming to fruition. There are soooo many great things inside and out to smile about!

Empowered to A.C.T.:

What inspired **ACTION** will you take today?
What purposeful **CHANGE** will you make today?
What can you **TEACH** someone else today?

Happy Smiling So Big Your Cheeks Hurt!

Remember, nothing happens until you decide to take action!

Today's Featured Reader:
Linda Ryan, Bridgewater, New Jersey
"I love this message, because it is such a great reminder, especially on the days when I am in a "funky" mood, that there's SO MUCH to be grateful for, even on my worst day. As a nurse I tend to be grateful for things like my kidneys, my liver, my heart, my lungs, my pancreas, my stomach, my esophagus, my gall bladder and my skin …Imagine if your SKIN didn't work?! I like to even go a step further and FEEL GRATITUDE for all the things that did NOT happen, like falling down the steps, or spilling my coffee, or getting a flat tire, or …fill in the blank!
Thank you Melissa for this much needed reminder!"

Be Your Own Picasso

"When I was a child, my mother said to me, 'If you become a soldier, you'll be a general. If you become a monk you'll end up as the pope.'
Instead I became a painter and wound up as Picasso."
~ Pablo Picasso

I love this quote! It seems like we always want to become someone else. We're always looking up to someone or putting someone on that proverbial pedestal. Don't get me wrong, it's great to have mentors in your life and we can learn a lot from them. But always remember how great YOU already are. You are special and unique. As a coach, I work with many people who are always comparing themselves to someone else. They think if they are more like that other person that their life will be better. I'm here to say the contrary; the more you are yourself, the better life will be. Be yourself. Like Picasso, just BE who YOU are and you will wind up being something GREAT!

⌐ Empowered to A.C.T.: ⌐

What inspired **ACTION** will you take today?
What purposeful **CHANGE** will you make today?
What can you **TEACH** someone else today?

Happy BEING YOU!

Remember, nothing happens until you decide to take action!

263

September

Get Started Right Where You Are!

"Your present circumstances don't determine where you can go;
they merely determine where you start."
~ Nido Qubein

The results you're currently getting in your life are just a snapshot and reflection of what you have been creating up until this point. They are by no means a determining factor of what you're able to create going forward. You can choose right here right now to create new circumstances for yourself. The power is always in this present moment. If that's what you want, then you get started from exactly where you are. If you want to save some money, you start by saving what you can right now whether it is $1 or $100 or more. If want to get in shape, you start by exercising what you can do right now whether it is working out 10 minutes or 60 minutes. Time to get started!

⁓ Empowered to A.C.T.: ⁓

What inspired **ACTION** will you take today?
What purposeful **CHANGE** will you make today?
What can you **TEACH** someone else today?

Happy Happiness in the Present!

Remember, nothing happens until you decide to take action!

Dream Big!

"The size of your success is measured by the strength of your desire; the size of
your dream; and how you handle disappointment along the way."
~ Robert Kiyosaki

Do you like to dream BIG? Do you like to close your eyes and imagine a lifestyle
that is full of joy, freedom and abundance? The magnitude to which the image you
hold in your mind will be fulfilled greatly depends on the strength of your desire
and your ability to handle the journey along the way. The journey is not always
a smooth ride, so your ability to be flexible and to stay strong through adversity,
disappointments, and setbacks is critical. Your rock solid, unwavering desire is
what will help you get through all those "bumps in the road." Your desire to be,
do, and create more on this planet will keep you getting back up again and again.
Never lose your DESIRE—it's the hunger, the thirst for life! Without it, we stop
evolving as human beings.

—⌒ Empowered to A.C.T.: ⌒—

What inspired **ACTION** will you take today?
What purposeful **CHANGE** will you make today?
What can you **TEACH** someone else today?

Happy Hungry Desire!

Remember, nothing happens until you decide to take action!

Happiness Awaits You Right Now!

"Learn to enjoy every minute of your life. Be happy now. Don't wait for something outside of yourself to make you happy in the future. Think how really precious is the time you have to spend, whether it's at work or with your family.
Every minute should be enjoyed and savored."
~ Earl Nightingale

It's easy to be happy when everything is going our way, but what about when times are tough? In tough times, we often look to someone or something to fix it for us. In that moment, we are relying on something from the outside to make us happy. YOU are the only one that can really make you happy and that starts from the inside. Begin by taking responsibility for your own happiness. Look for the lessons in the tough times and find gratitude in the blessings you have already. Time is so precious. Enjoy every minute of it. Take a moment right now and reflect on a time in your life that really felt good; a vacation, your wedding day, the birth of your child, a promotion, whatever it is for you. See it, feel it, hear it ... How does that feel? Savor that moment and enjoy it. Keep it with you all week long and enjoy making new memories too!

⚬ Empowered to A.C.T.: ⚬

What inspired **ACTION** will you take today?
What purposeful **CHANGE** will you make today?
What can you **TEACH** someone else today?

Happy Being Happy Right Now!

Remember, nothing happens until you decide to take action!

Love is Life

"Where there is love there is life."
~ Mahatma Gandhi

Love IS life! Oooh, I love that! Love is at the core of who we really are and it is the fuel that feeds the human spirit. It's the bright light that burns within all of us! Without love, we have nothing. Our souls are empty. If you think about it, it's when we love something that we have the energy and courage to go fulfill more of our potential, serve in greater ways, go the extra mile, bend over backwards, and take more risks. Think about all the people, things, places you love in your life. Now think about how all that love fuels your spirit and makes you feel ALIVE! Love and live a little louder today and you'll feel the love inside your heart burn greater and brighter!

⊸ Empowered to A.C.T.: ∾

What inspired **ACTION** will you take today?
What purposeful **CHANGE** will you make today?
What can you **TEACH** someone else today?

Happy Life is Love!

Remember, nothing happens until you decide to take action!

Today is YOUR Day! Seize it!

"Positive thinkers get positive results because they appreciate the inestimable value of a day, this day, not the next day, but this day, and every day. Today offers at least sixteen waking hours that may be crammed full of opportunity, joy, excitement, and achievement."
~ Norman Vincent Peale

Think about how much more productive positive thinkers are each day. Not just because they have a better attitude than those negative thinkers, but also because they know how to make the most out of a moment. They see the power in the present moment and they DO something with it! They are not putting so much time and energy into non-serving thoughts that cause them to waste their precious time and energy. Decide to be positive today and make the most out of each and every moment you have been gifted with! Just imagine how much you'll get done today! Wahoo!

⟶ Empowered to A.C.T.: ⟵

What inspired **ACTION** will you take today?
What purposeful **CHANGE** will you make today?
What can you **TEACH** someone else today?

Happy Seizing Each Moment!

Remember, nothing happens until you decide to take action!

Don't Merely Exist... LIVE Life!

"The proper function of man is to LIVE, not to exist."
~ Jack London

Guess what … You can change the world today! Yes, yes you can! But you won't change the world by just merely existing. You must LIVE your life to the fullest with purpose and gratitude. The world is waiting on you to step up! You are here to create and do very special things. Can you hear your calling? Are you guided and following that calling? Or are you just going through the motions of life, waiting for the weekend and a paycheck, just hanging in there and making it through each day? You see, you have been GIFTED this beautiful experience of life specifically to express and share your calling and your purpose which have been placed in your heart. So what do you choose? To change the world today or to merely exist and be left "unblossomed" (I know that's not a word, but I decided to make it up!) See, I just changed the world … I created a new word! LOL!:)

— Empowered to A.C.T.: —

What inspired **ACTION** will you take today?
What purposeful **CHANGE** will you make today?
What can you **TEACH** someone else today?

Happy Changing the World Today!

Remember, nothing happens until you decide to take action!

It's the Little Things That Add Up!

"Never get tired of doing the little things for others. Sometimes those little things occupy the biggest part of their hearts."
~ Unknown

Don't underestimate your value and the positive impact you are able to make on people. Your words of encouragement and belief, your acts of service, and your thoughtfulness touch our hearts in a way that is absolutely priceless. Never think it doesn't matter or it goes unnoticed. More than you know, you are very significant in the lives you come in contact with! What can you do today for someone else? An act of service, a kind word or a thoughtful gesture are some examples. Make it a day where you create a heartfelt and meaningful moment with someone today.

Empowered to A.C.T.:

What inspired **ACTION** will you take today?
What purposeful **CHANGE** will you make today?
What can you **TEACH** someone else today?

Happy Keeping Up With the Little Things in Life!

Remember, nothing happens until you decide to take action!

Live the Dream!

"If this were a dream right now, would you act any differently?"
~ David Deida

One of my favorite things to say is "Live the Dream!" So if you were actually in your dreams right now, like you were actually living the life of your dreams … what would you do differently? How would you show up differently? How would you act differently? Who would you have to be? Call forth your persistence, patience, courage, passion, love, excitement, and whatever other amazing characteristics you dream of that are necessary to create your dream life. Call forth that part of you here and now in this present moment. Live your dreams right here and right now! Be your absolute BEST YOU!

⟶ Empowered to A.C.T.: ⟵

What inspired **ACTION** will you take today?
What purposeful **CHANGE** will you make today?
What can you **TEACH** someone else today?

Happy Living the Dream, My Friend!

Remember, nothing happens until you decide to take action!

Today's Featured Reader:
Donniece Greene-Smith, London, United Kingdom
"I love this Daily W.O.W! There are so many things we need to do in order to show up in this world and at times it can become overwhelming just thinking about it, but when I remember the significance of the present moment I can't help but feel joy, peace, love knowing that in that moment I can become all that I desire to be. I love the Daily W.O.W's that remind me to BE PRESENT!
Thanks, Melissa, for all you do!"

You Are a Gift!

"Life is a gift, and it offers us the privilege, opportunity, and responsibility to give something back by becoming more."
~ Anthony Robbins

Along with your LIFE being a gift, YOU are a gift too! You are a magnificent being with more gifts within you than you can even wrap your mind around. And you have not been given these wonderful gifts by accident or for no reason! The more you express them the more you become more of your greater self! I believe it's our responsibility as human beings to become our greatest selves and express it with the world! Look a little closer today at your gifts you have to share. Don't keep them hidden, don't be shy, but rather let them become more of your greater self and let them shine bright! The world will thank you for it!

⸺ Empowered to A.C.T.: ⸻

What inspired **ACTION** will you take today?
What purposeful **CHANGE** will you make today?
What can you **TEACH** someone else today?

Happy Sharing Your Gifts With the World!

Remember, nothing happens until you decide to take action!

Have Patience to Do it Over and Over Again!

"Have patience. All things are difficult before they become easy."
~ Saadi

Think waaay back ... yes, waaay back to the first time you learned how to tie your shoes ... to the first time you wrote your name ... to the first time you drove a car. Remember how challenging those tasks were. You had to be focused and determined to learn and face something that felt new, awkward, and unfamiliar. You had to be patient and try and try again, even when you didn't feel like it. But look at you now, you are practically on autopilot and can do all of these things without thinking. It was your consistent patience and effort that got you to where you can do things with your eyes closed, driving a car being the exception! Whatever it is that you are facing now that seems difficult to learn, stick with it. Know that your consistent patience is critical to something becoming easy.

⸺ Empowered to A.C.T.: ⸺

What inspired **ACTION** will you take today?
What purposeful **CHANGE** will you make today?
What can you **TEACH** someone else today?

Happy Patience!

Remember, nothing happens until you decide to take action!

Be Open to Life Unfolding ... Unexpectedly!

"We must be willing to let go of the life we planned
so as to have the life that is waiting for us."
~ E. M. Forester King

How many times have you planned a part of your life out to every detail? I know I have and I know that most times it doesn't work out exactly as planned. This happens in life and on the job. If you have ever been a project manager, you know exactly what I'm talking about! Now don't get me wrong, I'm a huge advocate of planning, yet I have also learned to be more OPEN to letting life unfold unexpectedly. It isn't always easy, but by being open and allowing life to unfold, it's amazing what new opportunities, experiences, and relationships come into your life that you previously hadn't "planned" for.

—◦ Empowered to A.C.T.: ◦—

What inspired **ACTION** will you take today?
What purposeful **CHANGE** will you make today?
What can you **TEACH** someone else today?

Happy Planning ... and then Letting Go of the Plan!

Remember, nothing happens until you decide to take action!

Excellence is Calling Your Name!

"The important thing is this: to be able at any moment to sacrifice what we are for what we could become."
~ Charles DuBois

We have a tendency of getting a wee bit too comfortable hanging around in mediocrity because it's safe and uneventful. What kind of life is that though? Boooooooring! No, thanks! It's time to surrender the person that was created by your conditions and circumstances and become your true authentic self. Set yourself free to BECOME who you were meant to be. Take a stand and reach for the REAL you. It lies deep down inside and it's screaming to get out. Can you hear? It's trying to get your attention. If you be still and listen, you'll hear EXCELLENCE calling your name! Leave mediocrity behind once and for all and step up to become the excellent and magnificent YOU!

⤳ Empowered to A.C.T.: ⤶

What inspired **ACTION** will you take today?
What purposeful **CHANGE** will you make today?
What can you **TEACH** someone else today?

Happy Excellence!

Remember, nothing happens until you decide to take action!

278

Focus on Living in the Present

"Security in a relationship lies neither in looking back to what it was, nor forward to what it might be, but living in the present and accepting it as it is now."
~ Anne Morrow Lindbergh

Relationships require soooo much presence! If you are too focused on the past or the future, you miss out on embracing, loving, and growing in the moment you're in right here right now. Many relationships don't work out for this reason specifically—not living in and focusing on the moment being experienced. People are busy rehashing the past, which can't be changed and worrying about the future, which isn't even here yet, all while missing out on this moment. Think about your most important relationships. How can you focus more on what's going on now versus the past or future? How can you accept where the relationship is presently? Set your intention to create great joy and love in this moment—not tomorrow or the next day, but today, right now.

~ Empowered to A.C.T.: ~

What inspired **ACTION** will you take today?
What purposeful **CHANGE** will you make today?
What can you **TEACH** someone else today?

Happy Present Relationships!

Remember, nothing happens until you decide to take action!

Be a Hungry Learner!

"Always desire to learn something useful."
~ Sophocles

Do you have a hunger for learning? I know I do! I love learning new things, especially things that I'll be able to put to use that will make my life and others' lives better. One of my biggest weaknesses is buying books on Amazon.com. I have a stack of books waiting to be read. I just want to read so many things! I'm also already signed up for four upcoming seminars. I just love learning so much that sometimes I even bite off more than I can chew! How about you? What do you love to learn that is useful and makes a big difference in your life?

⌐ Empowered to A.C.T.: ⌐

What inspired **ACTION** will you take today?
What purposeful **CHANGE** will you make today?
What can you **TEACH** someone else today?

Happy Hungry Learner!

Remember, nothing happens until you decide to take action!

Never Work Another Day in Your Life

"Choose a job you love and you will never have to work a day in your life."
~ Confucius

When you are doing what you love and loving what you do, how can you go wrong? Not only are you loving live, you also will have a tremendous amount of gratitude for the life you have created. I look at my life and I am so beyond grateful for the work I get to do. I feel honored and privileged! That gratitude then fuels me to keep going strong, to get better at my craft, and serve in even greater ways. What do you love to do? How can you be even more grateful for it being your livelihood? If you're still stuck in a job you hate I am hoping this quote and my commentary will help motivate you to get rocking. Go to your job of course, but start planning one thing that will bring you closer to your dream and do it. Soon you'll have the job you love and you will never work another day in your life.

⌐ Empowered to A.C.T.: ⌐

What inspired **ACTION** will you take today?
What purposeful **CHANGE** will you make today?
What can you **TEACH** someone else today?

Happy Never Working Another Day In Your Life!

Remember, nothing happens until you decide to take action!

Enjoy the Journey

"One of the best things you can do for yourself as a learner is to cultivate the ability to value and enjoy the process of growth. It is going to take a long time, so you might as well enjoy the journey."
~ John C. Maxwell

I know at times we all wish we could snap our fingers and bypass the "journey" and just get to our destination. That may sound nice, but it's really the journey that allows us to actually appreciate and enjoy the destination; the effort, the determination, the highs, the lows, the people you meet along the way. All of it is what makes the destination so sweet! I know the journey is not always a smooth ride, but what if you knew there would be a day where you would look back on that hard time and you could appreciate it for what it was and you could see that it made you even more of who you are. We can never acknowledge nor appreciate those times if we aren't in it for the long haul. Be committed and enjoy the ride!

⚘ Empowered to A.C.T.: ⚘

What inspired **ACTION** will you take today?
What purposeful **CHANGE** will you make today?
What can you **TEACH** someone else today?

Happy Journey!

Remember, nothing happens until you decide to take action!

You Are Forever Changed!

"Problems never leave us the way they found us."
~ Robert H. Schuller

Take a look at who you are here and now. You are not the same person you were twelve months ago, six months ago, or even just a short three months ago. You have evolved with your life experiences … both the good ones and the not so good ones. You are forever changed! The beauty in every experience you have is that it gives you the opportunity to learn more about yourself; your inner blocks and barriers as well as your gifts, talents, and purpose. I invite you to go forward with a new perspective of your problems and setbacks. Change the way you look at them. Reflect on them and see them as a way to learn more about yourself, to break through a barrier and to fall in love with your gifts, talents, and purpose all over again!

◦ Empowered to A.C.T.: ◦

What inspired **ACTION** will you take today?
What purposeful **CHANGE** will you make today?
What can you **TEACH** someone else today?

Happy New Perspectives on Your Life!

Remember, nothing happens until you decide to take action!

The Law of Awareness

"The Law of Awareness: You must know yourself to grow yourself."
~ John C. Maxwell

Ahhh, my favorite Law of Growth! I know in my heart that my purpose for being here on this beautiful planet of ours is to widen and expand self-awareness so that you can know more of your greater purpose, truth and potential. As you become more and more aware of who you really are and your purpose in life, life becomes sweeter and more fulfilling! Unfortunately, our society doesn't encourage us to expand our self-awareness, but rather we are just expected to conform and follow the status quo. What school offers a "Discover Your Purpose" class? None! But they ALL should! Therefore it is up to us to do the inner work and grow from the INSIDE OUT so that we can lead purposeful and fulfilling lives. It's up to YOU! What inner work will you do today?

⟶ Empowered to A.C.T.: ⟵

What inspired **ACTION** will you take today?
What purposeful **CHANGE** will you make today?
What can you **TEACH** someone else today?

Happy Getting to Know Yourself!

Remember, nothing happens until you decide to take action!

Let Love Flow Like a River

"Love is not something you generate. It is something that you allow to flow through you. You have only to allow it to flow in order to experience its wonder."
~ Owen Waters

What if you could have even more love in your life than you already do? Guess what? You can! You ARE LOVE and it is just a matter of allowing more of your own love to pour out of you, as well as, allow more of it to flow in. Take a nice deep breath, close your eyes, and feel your heart open up. Imagine a big, bright, and warm light shining out of your chest and onto others. See this big, bright, and warm light everywhere and in everyone. On the inhale, take in all that love and light, and on the exhale express and share it with everyone. Remember, you ARE LOVE and love is all around you at all times. Just open yourself up to being it and let it flow like a river!

⟜ Empowered to A.C.T.: ⟞

What inspired **ACTION** will you take today?
What purposeful **CHANGE** will you make today?
What can you **TEACH** someone else today?

Happy BEING Love!

Remember, nothing happens until you decide to take action!

Are You a Priority?

"Make yourself a priority, not an option."
~ Unknown

What happens when you make yourself a priority? You consider your well-being and you make choices that honor and serve your desire for harmony, health, and happiness in your life. And then what happens when you have harmony, health, and happiness in your life? You have more energy to serve others and live positively, productive, and purposeful, don't you? Making yourself a priority is NOT about being selfish! It's NOT about neglecting others, but rather it's about taking care of yourself so that you can be of greater service and make a bigger difference in the world.

⌐ Empowered to A.C.T.: ⌐

What inspired **ACTION** will you take today?
What purposeful **CHANGE** will you make today?
What can you **TEACH** someone else today?

Happy Making Yourself a Priority!

Remember, nothing happens until you decide to take action!

Experience Your Potential Through Your Setbacks

*"Life's challenges are not supposed to paralyze you,
they're supposed to help you discover who you are."*
~ Bernice Johnson Reagon

What kind of meaning are you giving your challenges, failures, and setbacks? Do you define those experiences as defeats? Or do you define them as opportunities to discover more of who you really are and what you're made of? It's all in how you define and give meaning to it. Meaning is everything; it creates your reality. See it as a defeat and you'll get in your own way and hold yourself back. See it as an opportunity to experience more of your potential and you'll dust yourself off and give it another go. The more you keep forging ahead in life, the more and more you get to experience your true potential! You get to see just how powerful, resilient, and capable you really are! Life is sooo good, isn't it?!

⌁ Empowered to A.C.T.: ⌁

What inspired **ACTION** will you take today?
What purposeful **CHANGE** will you make today?
What can you **TEACH** someone else today?

Happy Experiencing Your True Potential!

Remember, nothing happens until you decide to take action!

What Does Your Future Hold?

"The best way to predict the future is to create it."
~ Dr. Forrest C. Shaklee

Do you ever wonder what tomorrow holds for you? Hmmm, well, you can start off by taking a look at your daily agenda! You see, you are a creator. Are you progressively creating, transforming, and growing toward your goal? What are you doing TODAY to ensure you create that goal? Where you spend your time, energy, and money TODAY plays a big role in what TOMORROW holds for you. Be deliberate! Ask yourself, "What can I do TODAY, not tomorrow, and not Monday, but today to move me in the direction of creating my goal?"

⎯◇ Empowered to A.C.T.: ◇⎯

What inspired **ACTION** will you take today?
What purposeful **CHANGE** will you make today?
What can you **TEACH** someone else today?

Happy Creating Your Future!

Remember, nothing happens until you decide to take action!

Effective Communication is KEY!

"When angry, you will probably make a speech you will regret."
~ Unknown

It's far too common for effective communication go out the window and for unpleasant things to be said and done simply out of anger. Usually when someone is angry, the thoughts running through their mind are generally not very positive and, at times, not even rational. Next time you feel yourself getting hot under the collar, take a moment and BREATHE and gather your thoughts before you speak or do anything. Remember, you cannot take spoken words or actions back. It will serve you to stop, put your attitude in check, and process your thoughts. Remind yourself how critical effective communication really is in that kind of situation … and actually in every situation!

Empowered to A.C.T.:

What inspired **ACTION** will you take today?
What purposeful **CHANGE** will you make today?
What can you **TEACH** someone else today?

Happy Effective Communication!

Remember, nothing happens until you decide to take action!

Do You Face Your Blocks?

"Not everything that is faced can be changed.
But nothing can be changed until it is faced."
~ James Baldwin

This quote reminds me of the Serenity prayer. It reminds me that there are certain things I can change and other things that are outside of my control and I cannot change. However, it is my duty to honor my God-given purpose and face the things that I can change, even if it is painful or I am uncomfortable in doing so. Nothing will change until I am courageous enough to face it. I can complain, I can ignore it, I can wish it away; however, none of these things will really do anything except delay the inevitable. If you desire change in your life, it's time to face the block or barrier that's been getting in your way up until now. This is why I love being a coach so much. I get the privilege of working with people by breaking down those pesky barriers and participating in their breakthroughs and transformations! What an honor!

⟿ Empowered to A.C.T.: ⟿

What inspired **ACTION** will you take today?
What purposeful **CHANGE** will you make today?
What can you **TEACH** someone else today?

Happy Breaking Through Your Barriers!

Remember, nothing happens until you decide to take action!

Pity Party—No, Thank You!

"Feeling sorry for yourself, and your present condition, is not only a waste of energy but the worst habit you could possibly have."
~ Dale Carnegie

Ahh, pity parties! We've all had our fair share of pity parties, pouting, acting like a 5 year old, call it what you want, you know you've been there before. I believe the reason why Dale Carnegie says this is a "waste of energy" and the "worst habit you could possibly have" is because it's a totally unresourceful state to be in. It's an emotional state that says, "I'm a victim, I'm helpless, I am at the effect of my circumstances, it's so and so's fault, etc." With this level of thinking, someone isn't thinking of solutions, answers, or how to take constructive action. Of course we are all in this state from time to time, but to stay in this state for long periods of time is literally destructive to your mind, body, and spirit. Notice when you're there and snap yourself out of it! Go do something that will encourage, energize and inspire you right away! The power is always in the present moment, so decide to have an awesome party instead of a pity party!

⟶ Empowered to A.C.T.: ⟵

What inspired **ACTION** will you take today?
What purposeful **CHANGE** will you make today?
What can you **TEACH** someone else today?

Happy Awesome Party!

Remember, nothing happens until you decide to take action!

Create a Pulsating Desire

"Desire is the starting point of all achievement, not a hope, not a wish, but a keen pulsating desire which transcends everything."
~ Napoleon Hill

I hate to break the news to you, but hoping and wishing get you nowhere! When Napoleon Hill says you have to have a "keen pulsating desire" it makes me think of something that has a heartbeat—a pulse. And things that have a heartbeat and pulse are ALIVE! Your desire must BE ALIVE! Is your desire alive? If not, you may need to defibrillate your desire! Otherwise, when your desire dies, so does the chance of your dream coming true. Create daily practices that keep your desire ALIVE!

Empowered to A.C.T.:

What inspired **ACTION** will you take today?
What purposeful **CHANGE** will you make today?
What can you **TEACH** someone else today?

Happy Pulsating Desire!

Remember, nothing happens until you decide to take action!

Make the Best of Everything

"The happiest people don't have the best of everything,
they just make the best of everything they have."
~ Unknown

I find it funny how sometimes we make being happy much more complicated than it really is. It's all about perspective and attitude. Each of us possesses the power from within to make the best of any situation regardless of what is going on. Even in the most challenging of times, we can choose a perspective and attitude that is productive and serving. Yes, I know that sometimes that's easier said than done, however once you allow yourself to process the emotions that surface from a difficult situation, there's always the possibility of gratitude and a bright, compelling future ahead. It's up to you to be present to what's going on and choose to be grateful and focus on the hope for a brighter and more compelling future. A question you may want to ask yourself in the moment is, "How can I make the best of this situation?"

~ Empowered to A.C.T.: ~

What inspired **ACTION** will you take today?
What purposeful **CHANGE** will you make today?
What can you **TEACH** someone else today?

Happy Making the Best of Every Situation!

Remember, nothing happens until you decide to take action!

Feel and Release Your Fears

"Remember that fear always lurks behind perfectionism. Confronting your fears and allowing yourself the right to be human can, paradoxically, make you a far happier and more productive person."
~ David M. Burns

We all have fear in one form or fashion and as much as we would love to get rid of it and never be afraid of anything, that's not going to happen. Fear is just one of many human emotions. Instead of avoiding and wishing your fears away, how about facing them and loving yourself along the way? That may in and of itself sound scary, but it's really where your freedom and success are! Seek to understand your perfectionism; where does it come from … how does it make you feel … what would happen if you did something perfectly imperfect? Look at it this way, when you explore your fears and face them, then you put yourself in a position to release them and truly love yourself! Judging your fears and stuffing them back down to never be addressed actually causes them to stick around forever and continually pop up and prevent you from LIVING LIFE!

Empowered to A.C.T.:

What inspired **ACTION** will you take today?
What purposeful **CHANGE** will you make today?
What can you **TEACH** someone else today?

Happy Feeling and Releasing Your Fears!

Remember, nothing happens until you decide to take action!

Make It Your Own

"Reading furnishes the mind only with material and knowledge;
it is thinking that makes what we read ours."
~ John Locke

Don't read just for the sake of reading. Read to absorb and make the information personal and your own. When I read a book, I like to read the book as if the author was talking to me personally. I think to myself, "What message is here for me? What is the author trying to tell me?" Each of us may be receiving a different message from the same book and that's OK. The point is that you receive the message you were meant to receive and you do something with it. That message wasn't delivered to you for no reason. Make it your own by doing something with it that will improve your life.

⟶ Empowered to A.C.T.: ⟵

What inspired **ACTION** will you take today?
What purposeful **CHANGE** will you make today?
What can you **TEACH** someone else today?

Happy Improving Your Life!

Remember, nothing happens until you decide to take action!

Being Purpose Driven Always WINS!

"When one has a passionate sense of purpose, energy rises, obstacles become incidental, and perseverance wins out."
~ John C. Maxwell

I love talking about PURPOSE because when you decide to live your purpose, it gives you a burst of energy, a burst of confidence and courage, and a burst of perseverance! It's like the best dose of caffeine out there— and it's FREE and healthy! I also notice when I'm living purposefully that love, kindness, and enthusiasm just ooze right out of me effortlessly! I can't think of any other state you would want to be in! Take some time today to center yourself in your purpose. Let it drive you! Why do you do what you do? Why do you get out of bed in the morning? Those questions are NOT for your head to answer, but rather your HEART and SOUL to answer! Breathe into your heart and feel a great sense of purpose with everything you do today!

⟶ Empowered to A.C.T.: ⟵

What inspired **ACTION** will you take today?
What purposeful **CHANGE** will you make today?
What can you **TEACH** someone else today?

Happy Being Purpose Driven!

Remember, nothing happens until you decide to take action!

October

What Matters Most to You?

"Our lives begin to end the day we become silent about things that matter."
~ Martin Luther King

What do you value most in your life? Maybe it's your family, your health, your faith, or a specific movement or cause. Do you do your best to make it a priority in your life? When we give up and stop prioritizing what we say we value, what we stand for, and what we believe in, we begin to slowly die within. We lose that zest for life. Let's reignite what matters most in your life. Ask yourself, "What matters most to me? What do I stand for? What do I believe in?" These are all great questions to help you get the juices flowing. Once you reflect and answer them, ask yourself next, "How can I make what's important to me a priority in my life?" Your life will thank you for it!

⁓ Empowered to A.C.T.: ⁓

What inspired **ACTION** will you take today?
What purposeful **CHANGE** will you make today?
What can you **TEACH** someone else today?

Happy Living With Value!

Remember, nothing happens until you decide to take action!

You Must Be Dissatisfied!

"Seeking perfection is an aspect of the evolutionary force that lives through everyone. If the evolutionary impulse is ALIVE in you, so is dissatisfaction."
~ David Deida

Embrace your dissatisfaction, it's a good thing! It means you are not satisfied with being complacent, stuck, and not growing! It means your spirit is continually seeking ways to evolve and improve yourself and the world around you. It means you are looking for more ways to share your gifts and talents with others so you can make a difference. When we no longer long to reach, stretch, and grow internally and externally is when we stop evolving into the better versions of ourselves. And honestly, everyone misses out when that happens! You are special and here for a reason, so I encourage you to reach, stretch, and grow today and every day! Evolution depends on it!

—⚬ Empowered to A.C.T.: ⚬—

What inspired **ACTION** will you take today?
What purposeful **CHANGE** will you make today?
What can you **TEACH** someone else today?

Happy Evolving!

Remember, nothing happens until you decide to take action!

What is Your Potential?

"The potential of the average person is like the huge ocean unsailed, a new continent unexplored, a world of possibilities waiting to be released and channeled toward some great good."
~ Brian Tracy

You have more potential than your mind can even imagine! It's unlimited! I don't believe the human mind can truly even grasp what "unlimited" really means. To relate our unlimited potential to the vastness of the ocean or a continent is to limit our potential! However, I totally get Brian Tracy's point here because at least these physical things give our human mind something to see that is tangible so it can begin to get an idea of how great and massive our own potential within us really is! Take a few minutes today to really contemplate how much of your own potential you may be neglecting to express with the world AND what are you going to do about it? How can you start growing into and sharing more of your potential with the world?

⌐ Empowered to A.C.T.: ⌐

What inspired **ACTION** will you take today?
What purposeful **CHANGE** will you make today?
What can you **TEACH** someone else today?

Happy Expressing More of Your Potential!

Remember, nothing happens until you decide to take action!

The Hallmark of Excellence

"The hallmark of excellence, the test of greatness, is consistency."
~ Jim Tressel

Think about something you excel at. Maybe it's your profession or a sport, or maybe you have mastered a skillset or talent that serves you in many ways. Either way, if you look back to the first time you attempted it, I would venture to guess that you have come a long way. There was a time when you were just a beginner and you weren't as good at it as you are now. It was the time, energy, effort, and sometimes even the money that you put into it to get better and better that brought you to greatness! It didn't happen overnight, but yet it was your consistency that made it happen! You studied and practiced over and over again, day in and day out. Without your consistent effort, you wouldn't be where you are today.

⌁ Empowered to A.C.T.: ⌁

What inspired **ACTION** will you take today?
What purposeful **CHANGE** will you make today?
What can you **TEACH** someone else today?

Happy Excelling Through Consistent Effort!

Remember, nothing happens until you decide to take action!

We Are Emotional Creatures

"When dealing with people, remember you are not dealing
with creatures of logic, but creatures of emotion."
~ Dale Carnegie

We are all creatures of emotion and we will use logic to justify our feelings. Notice
how if you are not committed to either a relationship or a goal emotionally, it's
pretty difficult to keep your focus and attention on it. Your attention will stray
toward the thing that you are emotionally connected to. Whether you're dealing
with people or working on a goal, a positive emotional connection is key! Take
a look at your relationships and goals. Ask yourself, "How can I create more
of a positive emotional connection to this relationship/goal? How can I stir up
some passion, enthusiasm, and drive for it?" Watch your attitude toward that
relationship/goal soar as your positive emotional connection to it strengthens.

⸺ Empowered to A.C.T.: ⸺

What inspired **ACTION** will you take today?
What purposeful **CHANGE** will you make today?
What can you **TEACH** someone else today?

Happy Positive Emotional Connections!

Remember, nothing happens until you decide to take action!

303

Dance Your Heart Out!

"And those who were seen dancing were thought to be insane by those who could not hear the music."
~ Friedrich Nietzsche

Do you sing like a rock star when you're in the car? Do you catch the rhythm and find yourself bouncing to the beat when you're standing in line at the store and a good song catches your attention? Do you think that makes you crazy? No way, my friend! You're in the joy of the moment and living life. Go for it! If someone says you're crazy for merely enjoying life, stop for a moment and say a prayer for them. How sad it must be to live in so much fear of what others might think that you cannot hear the music of life. The same works for your goals in life too. Don't let anyone turn off the music to your dreams. Crank up the volume and belt out the tune of your desires! Send some love to the sane and keep on dancing, keep on singing ... and in my case, I'll keep shaking my tambourines!

⌐ Empowered to A.C.T.: ⌐

What inspired **ACTION** will you take today?
What purposeful **CHANGE** will you make today?
What can you **TEACH** someone else today?

Happy Dancing to the Music!

Remember, nothing happens until you decide to take action!

OCTOBER 7TH

Time to Step Up!

"If you want a chance, then take one."
~ Richard Rodney

We all want a chance in life, but no one is going to hand it over. You gotta go for it! You've got a chance right here, right now because the power always resides in the present moment. I know there's something you've been wanting to do, an opportunity you've been wanting to take, a new habit you've been wanting to create or maybe an old bad habit you've been wanting to break. It's sitting in the back of your mind and it pops up every few days. Well, now is the time to take a chance on it. You will never hit a home run if you don't swing the bat. This is your chance. Step up to the plate and go for it! I'm rooting for you!

⟶ Empowered to A.C.T.: ⟵

What inspired **ACTION** will you take today?
What purposeful **CHANGE** will you make today?
What can you **TEACH** someone else today?

Happy Taking a Chance On Yourself!

Remember, nothing happens until you decide to take action!

How To Connect With Others

"To connect with others in their world, you can't just live in your own world.
You have to link what you want to say to what others' needs are.
People don't remember what we think is important;
they remember what they think is important."
~ John C. Maxwell

Let's be honest, we all have needs and we all want to get our needs met. It's in our interest to find vehicles that fulfill our greatest needs, both internally and externally. With that said, when you are trying to connect with others and build a relationship with them, you must keep in mind what their needs are. What is most important to them? Why would they even listen to what you have to say? It's about them, not about you. When you know these answers, you can communicate in a way that addresses what they need and want most. This way they will be more engaged and more vested in the relationship as well as the desired outcome.

— Empowered to A.C.T.: —

What inspired **ACTION** will you take today?
What purposeful **CHANGE** will you make today?
What can you **TEACH** someone else today?

Happy Connecting at a Deeper Level and Serving Their Needs!

Remember, nothing happens until you decide to take action!

Give Thanks For All That You Have

"The best way to get what we want is to be grateful for what we already have."
~ Unknown

Are you in a state of gratitude for the blessings in your life, big and small, tangible and intangible? Or have you been finding yourself frustrated, angry, or resentful because you are focusing on all that you do not have? What you are focusing on matters! No matter how difficult things might seem in life, there is ALWAYS something to be grateful for. Yes, always! One of the most powerful practices I have implemented into my life is to truly be grateful for all that I have. It's only when I intensify my gratitude does all that I desire comes rushing my way. Think about how you can intensify your gratitude today. Giving thanks is not just about making a list, but rather it's about truly FEELING grateful. Take it to a whole new level!

Empowered to A.C.T.:

What inspired **ACTION** will you take today?
What purposeful **CHANGE** will you make today?
What can you **TEACH** someone else today?

Happy Endless Gratitude!

Remember, nothing happens until you decide to take action!

Never Lose Hope, My Friend!

"We must accept finite disappointment, but we must never lose infinite hope."
~ Martin Luther King

We all have our trials and tribulations and our setbacks and challenges in life. It can be difficult and disappointing at times, especially when something doesn't go the way we planned after working so hard at it. Unfortunately when this happens often enough, we tend to lose hope. No one can change the outcome of what happened, but you can choose to walk away with a priceless life lesson and gift that you gained and can take with you as you continue on your journey in life. If you don't have that spark of hope, you may never even look for the lesson and gift, you just stay stuck in the doom and gloom of your disappointment. Look for the lesson and gift to spark that infinite hope! It's there; you just have to look for it!

⁓ Empowered to A.C.T.: ⁓

What inspired **ACTION** will you take today?
What purposeful **CHANGE** will you make today?
What can you **TEACH** someone else today?

Happy Infinite Hope!

Remember, nothing happens until you decide to take action!

Negotiate a New Reality

"Reality is negotiable."
~ Tim Ferriss

What is reality anyways? It's not carved in stone, but rather it's an illusion, a story, a perception, a thought pattern you tell yourself. It's just as made up as a bedtime story you read your children … or every "reality" TV show out there. So if that's the case, then why do we get soooo caught up in the drama of our stories? Why not just tell yourself a new story and create a new reality, one that is much more serving and healthy? Could it be that simple? I believe that once you start challenging your thoughts and stories on a regular basis that you will create a new reality for yourself. You will begin to see your world differently and no longer live through your old reality anymore. So YES, it's that simple. It may not always be easy, but it's definitely simple! Every day deliberately challenge your thoughts, perceptions, and your stories and you will watch your reality change right before your eyes!

Empowered to A.C.T.:

What inspired **ACTION** will you take today?
What purposeful **CHANGE** will you make today?
What can you **TEACH** someone else today?

Happy New Realities!

Remember, nothing happens until you decide to take action!

Your Purpose and Vision is in Your Heart

"Your vision becomes clear when you look inside your heart. Who looks outside, dreams. Who looks inside, awakens."
~ Carl Jung

Boy, oh, boy, I really love this quote! Too often we get stuck in our heads when it comes to our visions and we seek answers outside of us. Our mind will race all day long trying to figure it out; however, IN-sight is found IN-side! You see, your heart knows all there is to know. When you look into your heart you connect with your soul, the purpose and vision of your highest and greatest self-resides there! So next time you are seeking clarity on your purpose and vision, get out of your head and look inside your heart. What is it saying to you? Where is it guiding you?

Empowered to A.C.T.:

What inspired **ACTION** will you take today?
What purposeful **CHANGE** will you make today?
What can you **TEACH** someone else today?

Happy Looking Inside Your Heart!

Remember, nothing happens until you decide to take action!

Going From Good to GREAT!

"Say 'No' to the good so you can say 'Yes' to the great. In fact, concentrating on merely good often prevents the great from showing up, simply because there is no time left in our schedules to take advantage of any additional opportunity."
~ Jack Canfield

I've coached many professionals who were doing pretty well in their professional lives, however; they were looking to do GREAT things in their professional lives. If you find yourself in the same boat of wanting to go from good to great, you can start by defining the difference for you between what is good and what is great. What does a good client look like? And what does a great client look like? You can do this for your personal life as well. What does a good relationship look like? And what does a great relationship look like? Once you have both sides defined, then start thinking about what you would need to do differently to have GREAT clients and have GREAT relationships. Think about how you need to raise your standards. What information do you need to gather? What qualifying questions do you need to ask? What might your plan be? Greatness won't happen by accident. It's up to you to create it in your life!

—◇ Empowered to A.C.T.: ◇—

What inspired **ACTION** will you take today?
What purposeful **CHANGE** will you make today?
What can you **TEACH** someone else today?

Happy Greatness!

Remember, nothing happens until you decide to take action!

Transformation

"The visioning process is always self-examination. It is never, 'God, I want this.
Make this happen.' It is always, 'What do I have to become to live
the vision, to manifest it, to reveal it?' The visioning process,
then, is a process of transformation of the individual."
~ Rev. Michael Beckwith

So often we attempt to reach a new bigger and better goal by being the same
old person who got us here. The YOU who got you here is not the you who will
get you where you want to go. You must reach, stretch, and grow into a greater
version of yourself. You must expand your thinking and your self-awareness.
You must see yourself in a greater light and see the capabilities, resources, and
opportunities available to you. Step into and embody the essence of your greater
self. BE that person from the minute you wake up to the minute you go to bed.
The greatest power is in the BECOMING MORE, not the DOING MORE.
Allow yourself to become that which you wish to create in your life. Only then
will you truly transform.

—⁊ Empowered to A.C.T.: ⁊—

What inspired **ACTION** will you take today?
What purposeful **CHANGE** will you make today?
What can you **TEACH** someone else today?

Happy Transformation!

Remember, nothing happens until you decide to take action!

Are You Leading by Example?

"The most valuable gift a leader can give is being a good example. More than anything else, employees want leaders whose beliefs and actions line up. They want good models who lead from the front."
~ John C. Maxwell

Your actions are a representation of your beliefs, so if your actions are not in alignment with your words, we know that you truly don't believe what you're saying. Let your actions speak volumes for what you truly believe in! Those who share your similar beliefs will follow you and be inspired by you! They will give you their blood, sweat, and tears because they too believe in what you believe in and they are proud to have you as their leader! If you are a leader, but not walking your talk, others will pick up on it real quick. We can spot a phony from a mile away! It's a turn off and it is toxic to your success! BE your beliefs! BE your message!

⸻ Empowered to A.C.T.: ⸻

What inspired **ACTION** will you take today?
What purposeful **CHANGE** will you make today?
What can you **TEACH** someone else today?

Happy Leading by Example!

Remember, nothing happens until you decide to take action!

Shortcut? What shortcut?

"There are no short cuts to any place worth going."
~ Beverly Sills

Want to know the shortcut to success? It's to STOP looking for a shortcut! That's the shortcut! We are all programmed by our environment to find the quick fix, the pill, that too-good-to-be-true shortcut that will get us out of having to do all the real work, to not have to really give it our all, and not be fully committed! I encourage you to fully commit yourself to your goals and dreams. Be willing to do the inner and outer work required to truly evolve and transform into the person you want to be. You'll grow more than you can imagine along the journey of mastering and accomplishing your heart's desire than you will if you take some "shortcut."

⟶ Empowered to A.C.T.: ⟵

What inspired **ACTION** will you take today?
What purposeful **CHANGE** will you make today?
What can you **TEACH** someone else today?

Happy TEAM!

Remember, nothing happens until you decide to take action!

Think Yourself Healthy

"You can promote your healing by your thinking."
~ James E. Sweeney

Not feeling well? Have you ever heard someone say they "worried themselves sick"? Well, it's true! You can actually create dis-ease in the body by negatively obsessing over something. Your thoughts are energy and negative thoughts are destructive and literally destroy the cells in your body. On the flip side, positive and loving thoughts can actually repair and build healthy cells in your body. Just think about the last time you were in a drawn-out heated argument. It was probably physically and emotionally draining and exhausting. On the flip side, think of the last time you had a really great day that you put a lot of love and care into. How did you feel? Probably stronger than ever and more energized. Yes, your thoughts impact your physiology and health! Direct your thoughts in a way that heal you and make you stronger!

⸻ Empowered to A.C.T.: ⸻

What inspired **ACTION** will you take today?
What purposeful **CHANGE** will you make today?
What can you **TEACH** someone else today?

Happy Healthy Thinking and Healing!

Remember, nothing happens until you decide to take action!

Shine Bright!

*"As we let our own light shine, we unconsciously give
other people permission to do the same."*
~ Nelson Mandela

You work hard. You accomplish things that make you proud. You wonder
sometimes if anyone even notices. Well, try this on for size. Shine the
spotlight on yourself and share your excitement about your achievements
and your journey getting there. Your old conditioning may tell you that
it's your ego wanting a boost. It very well may be, but consider this
... what if in sharing your accomplishments and the journey along the
way, you inspired someone else to set out and achieve their own goals?
What if it gave someone hope and encouragement? Would that be
worth it? When you shine your own light with the intention of helping
others, you give them permission to shine. Imagine the viral effect.
You could illuminate the planet.

⌐ Empowered to A.C.T.: ⌐

What inspired **ACTION** will you take today?
What purposeful **CHANGE** will you make today?
What can you **TEACH** someone else today?

Happy Shining Bright!

Remember, nothing happens until you decide to take action!

It's Time to Relax!

"The time to relax is when you don't have time for it."
~ Sydney J. Harris

'Tis the season for enormous to do lists. Ever catch yourself running around like a crazy person screaming for more time in the day, trying to get it all done. Sound familiar? If you want to get more done this season, then STOP. Choose to honor yourself in this moment and take some much deserved time for you. Not only do you deserve it, but it will make you more productive. Don't let your mind argue this point with you. If you are operating on empty or from a state of exhaustion, no one benefits. TODAY and each day forward, take some time to relax and rejuvenate. Your mind, body and spirit will thank you for it!

⌐ Empowered to A.C.T.: ¬

What inspired **ACTION** will you take today?
What purposeful **CHANGE** will you make today?
What can you **TEACH** someone else today?

Happy Relaxing!

Remember, nothing happens until you decide to take action!

What's Keeping You From Success?

"The greatest barrier to success is the fear of failure."
~ Sven Goran Erikson

The fear of failure is a very real feeling for all of us; however, within that fear is also where your success resides. That fear can seem like the greatest challenge you will ever face, but once you choose to face the fear and work through it, success is awaiting you! Choose to change your perception of your fears and look at them as an invitation to your growth and success. Take a moment right now and ask yourself, "Where in my life am I fearful?" and then re-ask the question by asking, "Where in my life am I being invited to grow and meet with success?"

⟶ Empowered to A.C.T.: ⟵

What inspired **ACTION** will you take today?
What purposeful **CHANGE** will you make today?
What can you **TEACH** someone else today?

Happy Invitation to Success!

Remember, nothing happens until you decide to take action!

The Law of Reflection

"The Law of Reflection: Learning to pause allows growth to catch up with you."
~ John C. Maxwell

John C. Maxwell is a dear friend and business partner of mine. I am honored to work with him and be in his presence. He has taught me so much. One of the many things I am grateful to him for teaching me is the power of reflection and how it's really an invaluable "law" of growth and development. He has taught me that it is only through reflection that we actually turn an experience into wisdom. Without the reflection, we may not gain the clarity and wisdom from that experience and we may repeat a mistake over and over again. Be sure to reflect regularly on your experiences. Learn and grow from them. Remember, without reflection, an experience is just an experience. It won't become wisdom nor serve your highest and greatest good until you take the time to reflect on what happened.

⁓ Empowered to A.C.T.: ⁓

What inspired **ACTION** will you take today?
What purposeful **CHANGE** will you make today?
What can you **TEACH** someone else today?

Happy Reflection!

Remember, nothing happens until you decide to take action!

Be Saved By Criticism!

"The trouble with most of us is that we would rather be
ruined by praise than saved by criticism."
~ Norman Vincent Peale

Boy, oh, boy, it feels great to receive praise! And boy, oh, boy, it can feel terrible to receive criticism! However, some criticism has good intentions and is meant to come from love and be an opportunity for you to see something about yourself that you previously weren't seeing. It may be an opportunity for you to reach, stretch, and grow. Sometimes it can be hard to hear and difficult to swallow, but it may just be exactly the tough love you need to propel you to the next level. Any time you receive criticism, stop and ask yourself, "Is there something here for me to learn from?" "Where can I grow?" You may be pleasantly surprised by the hidden gift!

⌒ Empowered to A.C.T.: ⌒

What inspired **ACTION** will you take today?
What purposeful **CHANGE** will you make today?
What can you **TEACH** someone else today?

Happy Criticism!

Remember, nothing happens until you decide to take action!

Master Your Thoughts

"Self-discipline begins with the mastery of your thoughts. If you don't control what you think, you can't control what you do. Simply, self-discipline enables you to think first and act afterward."

~ Napoleon Hill

Your thoughts control your every movement, act, and deed! Yes, your thoughts are that powerful! Think about it (ha, no pun intended), when you are thinking thoughts focused on your fear, doubt, stress, lack of time, lack of money, and lack of confidence, you usually don't take much action, if any at all! It's when you are in a peak mental state and you are thinking thoughts focused on your strengths, your faith, and the possibility of success that gets you out of your seat and excited to take action. Begin today to control and master your thoughts and when you do, your thoughts are going to serve you and take you much further in life!

⟶ Empowered to A.C.T.: ⟵

What inspired **ACTION** will you take today?
What purposeful **CHANGE** will you make today?
What can you **TEACH** someone else today?

Happy Mastering Your Thoughts!

Remember, nothing happens until you decide to take action!

Today's Featured Reader:
Mark Hernandez, Baytown, Texas
"I now realize that I am the master of my thoughts! One day I was filling out a new social security card form, when I came to place on the form where it asked for my father's name, date of birth, and social. It wasn't until I marked "unknown" that I felt a cold feeling and a voice say, "You have no name and no identity." I was raised by my step-father since I was 11 years old. I have not seen my paternal father. At that moment, a negative thought entered my mind, but I was able to not allow it to enter my HEART. For the first time, I beat that thought with the power of self-discipline; from I can't to I CAN! Thank you Melissa!"

Embrace Where You Are!

"Did you know that you are right where you are supposed to be?"
~ David Arch

There is something I know for sure and that is that you and I are exactly where we are supposed to be in life. Let go of the idea that you are supposed to be somewhere else. There's great purpose for you in this moment, regardless of whether you are dealing with an obstacle, setback, disappointment, or a great success and happiness. It doesn't matter if you are in a peak or a valley, you are supposed to be there to learn and grow from that exact experience. Stop running from it and find the greater purpose in it. You'll learn and grow more than you ever imagined if you choose to embrace where you are.

Empowered to A.C.T.:

What inspired **ACTION** will you take today?
What purposeful **CHANGE** will you make today?
What can you **TEACH** someone else today?

Happy Connecting to Your Happy Embracing Right Where You Are!

Remember, nothing happens until you decide to take action!

Are You Destined to Succeed?

"Some people succeed because they are destined to, but
most people succeed because they are determined to."
~ Unknown

Doesn't it seem like some people have success handed to them while others work
so hard at it? I believe those who seem to have success handed to them **DO NOT**
have it as easy as we may think. I believe they are truly committed and determined
to succeed just as those who are working so hard. I believe true success comes from
within. You must have the mindset and attitude that matches success. Miserable,
negative, and doubtful people are usually not the most successful. It's those who
are purposeful, positive, passionate, and determined make it to the top and stay
there. The type of mindset and attitude you embody either lifts you up or drags
you down and that plays a huge part in how you show up, your activity, and
results! Choose to embody a state that lifts you up and it will appear as though you
were destined to succeed all along!

⟶ Empowered to A.C.T.: ⟵

What inspired **ACTION** will you take today?
What purposeful **CHANGE** will you make today?
What can you **TEACH** someone else today?

Happy Destined to Succeed!

Remember, nothing happens until you decide to take action!

The Law of Curiosity

"The Law of Curiosity: Growth is stimulated by asking WHY?"
~ John C. Maxwell

Why do you think young children learn so much so quickly ... because they ask "WHY?" all day long! They are in a beautiful state of curiosity. They don't assume they have all the answers and they aren't embarrassed to ask whatever question is on their mind. Children are great teachers for us, aren't they?! My mentor, business partner, and friend, John C. Maxwell has taught me that it's only when I am asking questions, both internally and externally, am I learning something. How often are you asking questions that will stimulate your learning and growth? Begin to ask GREAT questions and you'll get GREAT answers! The more thought provoking question, the more insightful answer!

⟶ Empowered to A.C.T.: ⟵

What inspired **ACTION** will you take today?
What purposeful **CHANGE** will you make today?
What can you **TEACH** someone else today?

Happy Asking Quality Questions!

Remember, nothing happens until you decide to take action!

Express Your Gratitude

"Gratitude, left unshared, is like a gift that is wrapped and never given."
~ Unknown

How many times in the last few weeks have you felt grateful for something someone has done for you and you didn't express sincere appreciation in some way? Letting others know how much we appreciate them sends forth a string of positive energy whose influence is far reaching. Everyone feels good all around! The wonderful thing is that each of us possesses the power from within to make a difference today, and every day, by expressing our thanks for the many kind things others do for us. Today I am going to invite you to thank at least three people for something they did or are doing.

⁓ Empowered to A.C.T.: ⁓

What inspired **ACTION** will you take today?
What purposeful **CHANGE** will you make today?
What can you **TEACH** someone else today?

Happy Gratitude!

Remember, nothing happens until you decide to take action!

Are You Insane?

"There is nothing that is a more certain sign of insanity than to do the same thing over and over and expect the results to be different."
~ Albert Einstein

This quote is so true, so simple and so logical to understand, yet so many people get stuck in the pattern of insanity! Let's say you have this strong desire to harvest tomatoes, but you keep planting corn. Could you imagine planting corn seeds again and again and wondering why on earth you're not harvesting tomatoes! That would be insane, right?! Be willing to be honest with yourself and take a good look and see where you might be acting a wee bit insane. The first step in regaining your sanity is always awareness! Become aware of where your thoughts, feelings, and actions are not in alignment with your true desires!

─◌ Empowered to A.C.T.: ◌─

What inspired **ACTION** will you take today?
What purposeful **CHANGE** will you make today?
What can you **TEACH** someone else today?

Happy Sanity!

Remember, nothing happens until you decide to take action!

What is a Perfect Affirmation?

"You don't need to worry about finding the perfect affirmation, because
if you affirm something that's positive and feels good, then it will be
the perfect affirmation for that moment!"
~ Holly Baer

Affirmations are a great way to help us direct our thoughts. However, so often I
hear how much time is spent on fixing and tweaking affirmations to be just perfect,
when really they don't require all that much work to be perfect. All you have to do
is find the words that shift your energy in that moment; words that lift you up and
keep you going and moving forward. Whatever words help you shift to a higher and
better place, are the perfect words! Who knows, those words you use may change 10
minutes from now, and then tomorrow the words may change again. That's totally
fine. What matters is that you are feeling uplifted, energized, inspired, and action
driven! Affirm whatever you have to affirm to get into that peak state.

─◦ Empowered to A.C.T.: ◦─

What inspired **ACTION** will you take today?
What purposeful **CHANGE** will you make today?
What can you **TEACH** someone else today?

Happy Peak State Affirmations!

Remember, nothing happens until you decide to take action!

Go Ahead, Try Something New!

"Never be afraid to try something new. Remember, amateurs built the ark. Professionals built the *Titanic*."

~ Unknown

I know you've got something tucked safely away that you have wanted to try. You have an idea or a thought that has been nudging you to "give it a go." You even may have something you started, but it wasn't going quite as planned so you quickly stuffed it back into "safe keeping." Big mistake. Don't tuck away those things you want to try. It's those things that are an expression of your true self and give you a greater sense life. It's those things that will get your juices flowing and propel you to success and fulfillment. Even the pros were amateurs at one time. You will never hit a home run from the sidelines watching the game. Unpack those things you've tucked "safely" away today. They don't belong in the baggage compartment, they belong in flight!

⟋ Empowered to A.C.T.: ⟍

What inspired **ACTION** will you take today?
What purposeful **CHANGE** will you make today?
What can you **TEACH** someone else today?

Happy Trying Something New!

Remember, nothing happens until you decide to take action!

Interrupt the Mind Chatter!

"The ability to be in the present moment is a
major component of mental wellness."
~ Abraham Maslow

Doesn't it just drive you crazy sometimes when your mind is all over the place? It's thinking about the past, then the future, then the past again … AARGGH! I know it surely drives me crazy! I call this mind chatter. It's when you have a difficult time focusing on the present moment because there's all this chatter going on in your mind about everything BUT the present! When I catch myself stuck in this mind chatter state, I take a nice big deep breath and call myself into the present moment. I step back from whatever experience I'm having and be an observer of it. I assess what's really going on and look for how I can maximize and fulfill the present moment. I am in much more resourceful state when I'm present versus when my mind is all over the place. Try it out yourself. It's a great way to feel empowered in the present moment and not give into all that mental chaos!

─◌ Empowered to A.C.T.: ◌─

What inspired **ACTION** will you take today?
What purposeful **CHANGE** will you make today?
What can you **TEACH** someone else today?

Happy Interrupting the Mind Chatter!

Remember, nothing happens until you decide to take action!

November

Do You Accept Responsibility?

"There two primary choices in life: to accept conditions as they exist, or accept the responsibility for changing them."
~ Denis Waitley

Nobody is going to go out there and create the perfect life FOR YOU. You either accept the cards you have been dealt or you ask for a new hand. I say, ask for a new hand if you are unhappy! You can design and create a life you truly desire for yourself and your family. There's no need to complain about current conditions and circumstances in your life ... just accept responsibility for changing them. You know you have the power to change and transform your current situation ... you know that, right?! So do what you need to do to get a new outcome. Transformation begins with YOU!

Empowered to A.C.T.:

What inspired **ACTION** will you take today?
What purposeful **CHANGE** will you make today?
What can you **TEACH** someone else today?

Happy Accepting Responsibility For Your Life!

Remember, nothing happens until you decide to take action!

Be As Grateful As a Dog!

"Does not the gratitude of the dog put to shame
any man who is ungrateful to his benefactors?"
~ Saint Basil

Ha, ha! I love this quote! It's so true! I love how dogs always make you feel like you're the best thing on the planet. They're not afraid to show you much love and gratitude. They definitely put to shame any ungrateful humans. The other thing I love about dogs and gratitude is that not only do they not hold back, they also do it effortlessly! They aren't "trying" to be grateful and loving, they just ARE. They are constantly in an effortless state of gratitude! How can we learn to emulate dogs by not holding back our love and gratitude and also showing it effortlessly? That's my challenge to you today. Go out there and be as grateful and loving as a dog is and make it EASY peasy!

─◠ Empowered to A.C.T.: ◡─

What inspired **ACTION** will you take today?
What purposeful **CHANGE** will you make today?
What can you **TEACH** someone else today?

Happy Being As Grateful As a Dog!

Remember, nothing happens until you decide to take action!

Lead with Love Today and Every Day!

"I have decided to stick with love. Hate is too great a burden to bear."
~ Martin Luther King, Jr.

Hatred is heavy and exhausting! It takes everything you've got to carry hate around with you! Not to mention it's toxic; hatred is destructive to relationships and life in general. Love on the other hand is so light and energizing that at times you feel like you're floating and yet full of energy! Have you used the term "cloud nine" when you refer to being in love? YES, that's totally how it feels, isn't it? So why not choose to feel that way toward everyone and everything?! Imagine how amazing you would feel all the time if you came from a place of love with everything you did. Not only would you feel amazing, you'd also be contributing to everyone else feeling amazing! Lead with love today … and every day!

— Empowered to A.C.T.: —

What inspired **ACTION** will you take today?
What purposeful **CHANGE** will you make today?
What can you **TEACH** someone else today?

Happy Leading with Love!

Remember, nothing happens until you decide to take action!

True Leadership is Earned

"True leadership cannot be awarded, appointed, or assigned. It comes only from influence, and that cannot be mandated. It must be earned."
~ John C. Maxwell

Just because someone has been assigned a big fancy title does not make them a great leader. I'm sure everyone at one time or another has experienced a poor leader with a big fancy title before. The big fancy title does not mean you respect that person or that you believe what they believe. It merely means they are in a position of authority that was assigned to them. Those who have developed and earned their leadership role are the ones who have earned your respect and inspire you to want to follow them—not because you have to, but because YOU want to. Now that's influence!

⌐ Empowered to A.C.T.: ⌐

What inspired **ACTION** will you take today?
What purposeful **CHANGE** will you make today?
What can you **TEACH** someone else today?

Happy Influencing and Inspiring Through True Leadership!

Remember, nothing happens until you decide to take action!

We Are a TEAM!

"There are no problems we cannot solve together,
and very few that we can solve by ourselves."
~ Lyndon B. Johnson

We are powerful spiritual beings that have been gifted with an intellect and
beautiful body to live in. The power within us was put there so you and I could
make a purposeful difference in the world. The interesting thing is that we were
not meant to live out our purposes alone! You and I are meant to change the world
TOGETHER! When we collaborate and bring our gifts and talents together,
we are able to tap into greater resources than by just going at it alone. You and
I multiply the number of ideas and solutions when we come together and form
a team! Work WITH someone today on a special project. Collaborate and create
something 10 times more amazing, life changing, and purposeful!

Empowered to A.C.T.:

What inspired **ACTION** will you take today?
What purposeful **CHANGE** will you make today?
What can you **TEACH** someone else today?

Happy TEAM!

Remember, nothing happens until you decide to take action!

Believe In Your Success

"Success is easy—after you believe—and since you are on your way to believing, you are on your way to succeeding."

~ Zig Ziglar

We like to make success so much more complicated than necessary. Many times we aren't missing but one key ingredient to success; BELIEF! When you begin to truly believe in yourself and your potential, success will come rushing toward you so fast you won't know what to do with it. One major block to belief is that many people get caught in the "Maybe Zone." Maybe it will work and maybe it won't. The "Maybe Zone" is a dangerous place to be because you never truly make significant and lasting progress. You're up one day and down the next. Create more consistent belief in yourself by getting out of the "Maybe Zone" and into the "Certainty Zone!" Have certainty that you will be and are successful! See it, feel it, touch it! Create a new identity of certainty for yourself!

⁓ Empowered to A.C.T.: ⁓

What inspired **ACTION** will you take today?
What purposeful **CHANGE** will you make today?
What can you **TEACH** someone else today?

Happy Believing with Certainty in YOU and Your Success!

Remember, nothing happens until you decide to take action!

Choose Better Feeling Thoughts

"The more you deliberately choose better-feeling thoughts, the more easy and ready to access you will have to those thoughts."
~ Esther Hicks (the Teachings of Abraham)

Your mind is like a physical muscle. The more your exercise it, the stronger it becomes. When you exercise your ability to choose your thoughts and you deliberately choose better-feeling thoughts over not-so-good-feeling thoughts, you find yourself more easily accessing the thoughts that lift you up and energize you rather than the ones that drain you and drag you down. Develop your MIND muscle! Exercise it day by day and moment by moment to serve you rather than work against you. If you want to get out of your own way, your mind must access thoughts that encourage and support you to express more of your God-given purpose and talents.

⟶ Empowered to A.C.T.: ⟵

What inspired **ACTION** will you take today?
What purposeful **CHANGE** will you make today?
What can you **TEACH** someone else today?

Happy Better-Feeling Thoughts!

Remember, nothing happens until you decide to take action!

Are You a Great Leader?

"The higher you want to climb, the more you need leadership. The greater the impact you want to make, the greater your influence needs to be. Without leadership ability, a person's impact is only a fraction of what it could be with good leadership."
~ John C. Maxwell

Since becoming business partners with John C. Maxwell and joining the faculty of the John C. Maxwell Team, I have been having a great time widening my awareness of the true power of great leadership. I can see how great leadership is truly the way to more effectively share your purpose with the world and make a greater difference! The catch is that until you raise your "leadership lid" you will always be limited in the difference and impact you are able to make. The greater your ability to lead others effectively will determine the potential impact you can have on your organization/team/family/community. How effective of a leader are you? How can you develop and take your leadership skills to the next level? Don't miss out on the opportunity to make an even greater difference both personally and professionally!

⌐ Empowered to A.C.T.: ⌐

What inspired **ACTION** will you take today?
What purposeful **CHANGE** will you make today?
What can you **TEACH** someone else today?

Happy Raising Your Leadership Lid!

Remember, nothing happens until you decide to take action!

Create Your Greatest Desires

"When your desires are different than your beliefs,
you will always create your beliefs."
~ Les Brown

The thoughts you believe in become your reality. Not the thoughts you WANT to believe in, but the ones you actually believe in. You are a phenomenal creator, I guarantee it. You create every single day of your life. If you aren't seeing what you desire in your life, examine your true beliefs. What do you really believe? Be honest with yourself. Do you really believe that you can have what you REALLY want or do you believe it's not possible or too far-fetched? If you are going to be creating anyway, why not create your greatest desires?

⟿ Empowered to A.C.T.: ⟿

What inspired **ACTION** will you take today?
What purposeful **CHANGE** will you make today?
What can you **TEACH** someone else today?

Happy Creating Your Greatest Desires!

Remember, nothing happens until you decide to take action!

Breathe Belief Into Yourself!

"You may succeed if no one believes in you, but you will never succeed
if you don't believe in yourself."
~ Unknown

Ahhh, the beautiful power of self-belief! You can move mountains when you
believe in yourself! Think about it ... When you believe in yourself you see
yourself and the whole world differently. You see your potential. You see the
possibilities rather than the limitations. You don't let setbacks hold you back
or define you. You have a sense of knowing and certainty. You are not a victim
of outside naysayers or circumstances. Let's face it, when you believe in yourself
life is just better! You're happier, more confident, and you believe in your ability
to change the world. Now come on, folks, isn't it worth it to develop your self-
belief? I'd say so! Create daily rituals that breathe belief into yourself, who you
are, your purpose for being here, and your marvelous gifts and talents! You are
magnificent ... believe it, my friend!

⟿ Empowered to A.C.T.: ⟿

What inspired **ACTION** will you take today?
What purposeful **CHANGE** will you make today?
What can you **TEACH** someone else today?

Happy Believing in Yourself!

Remember, nothing happens until you decide to take action!

YOU are a Genius

"Everybody is a genius. But if you judge a fish by its ability to climb a tree,
it will live its whole life believing that it is stupid."
~ Albert Einstein

Are you comparing yourself again? Stop it already! If you live your life comparing
yourself to others, I guarantee, you will find someone better at something than you
are. When we compare ourselves to others, we are usually comparing our weakest
points to their strongest thus setting ourselves up for disappointment. You are a
genius. You have the greatest gifts and no one can express them like YOU can.
You are one of a kind! Revel in your gifts. Develop them to an even greater level.
Share them with the world. From there, you will find joy, enthusiasm and peace.

Empowered to A.C.T.:

What inspired **ACTION** will you take today?
What purposeful **CHANGE** will you make today?
What can you **TEACH** someone else today?

Happy Being a Genius!

Remember, nothing happens until you decide to take action!

Embrace Who and Whose You Are!

"The art of life is to live in the present moment, and to make that moment as perfect as we can by the realization that we are the instruments and expression of God Himself."
~ Emmet Fox

Ahh, what a beautiful quote! I love love love knowing that I am an instrument and expression of God. Just that statement alone makes me appreciate even that much more the life I have been given along with the beauty of each moment. I see it as a privilege and honor to make the most of the present moment. Embrace who and whose you really are and make this very moment the best it can be.

— Empowered to A.C.T.: —

What inspired **ACTION** will you take today?
What purposeful **CHANGE** will you make today?
What can you **TEACH** someone else today?

Happy Making This Moment the Best it Can Be!

Remember, nothing happens until you decide to take action!

Reach, Stretch, Grow ... Always!

"Too many people stop learning because they have come to believe that you go through twelve years of school then you go to college for four years and then your education is over. But a good education really does nothing more than prepare you to stretch and learn for the rest of your life."
~ John C. Maxwell

Unfortunately, there are many people who resist change. They want to pay their dues and be done. But really, you and I are not meant to ever stop reaching, stretching, and growing ... EVER! Know that you can always learn more ... ALWAYS! If you think you "know it all" then you're missing out not only on many opportunities to live life more joyfully, but you are also robbing yourself of the joy of fully exercising and fulfilling your potential. Life gets really boring when you resist change and stop embracing reaching, stretching, and growing! How about you start reading a new book, find a mentor or coach you want to work with to help take you to the next level, sign up for a new fitness class, develop your hobbies and interests, grow your relationships, etc. Whatever it is, start today!

—⌒ Empowered to A.C.T.: ⌒—

What inspired **ACTION** will you take today?
What purposeful **CHANGE** will you make today?
What can you **TEACH** someone else today?

Happy Reaching, Stretching, and Growing for LIFE!

Remember, nothing happens until you decide to take action!

Be the Gratitude Leader

"Feeling gratitude isn't born in us—it's something we are taught,
and in turn, we teach our children."
~ Joyce Brothers

I love it when I encounter really polite and grateful children. It's a reflection of
their upbringing and whether their parents, teachers, and other guardians are
instilling in them the importance of feeling grateful and expressing it. The earlier
we can instill this in children the better. There are many adults out there who
really struggle with feeling and expressing gratitude. How can we change that?
Let's all begin encouraging our children and even other adults to feel and express
more gratitude. Tonight when you are sitting around the dinner table, go around
the table and ask everyone to share at least one thing they are grateful for. Do this
often enough so that it doesn't feel awkward sharing. You can try this at work
too. ask your team members to express thanks to at least one other team member.
Maybe they helped you with a project or solve a problem. Encourage them to
express their thanks! Be known as the Gratitude Leader!

⌐ Empowered to A.C.T.: ⌐

What inspired **ACTION** will you take today?
What purposeful **CHANGE** will you make today?
What can you **TEACH** someone else today?

Happy Being The Gratitude Leader!

Remember, nothing happens until you decide to take action!

A Loveless Life is Not An Option!

"Keep love in your heart. A life without it
is like a sunless garden when the flowers are dead."
~ Oscar Wilde

Just the thought of a loveless life sounds so pointless. Love is where it's at, my friend!
If you truly want to experience life, like really experience what life has to offer you,
then it's an absolute must that you keep love in your heart! Having love in your
heart means being compassionate, appreciative, and open to life. Do you have love
in your heart? I'm going to guess that's a big YES! Today my challenge to you is to
share and express it even more than you already do! Think of how you can be more
compassionate today, more appreciative, and more open to all that life brings you.

⌾ Empowered to A.C.T.: ⌾

What inspired **ACTION** will you take today?
What purposeful **CHANGE** will you make today?
What can you **TEACH** someone else today?

Happy Keeping Love in Your Heart!

Remember, nothing happens until you decide to take action!

Your Thoughts Become Your Emotions

"The emotions that drain you are the emotions that come from fear; the emotions that give you more energy are those that come from love."
~ Don Miguel Ruiz

Your thought patterns are what impact your emotions. You'll know which thoughts of yours are fear-based and which are love-based by how you feel emotionally. Throughout your day do you feel more energized and uplifted or do you feel more drained and dragged down? If you want to feel more energized, you can begin to shift your emotions to be more energizing and uplifting by shifting the source of your thoughts from fear to love. Your thoughts must originate from a place of love, desire, and passion rather than fear, lack, and pain. Be deliberate with this. Deliberately choose more loving and serving thoughts that you know will fulfill your highest and greatest good.

—∘ Empowered to A.C.T.: ∘—

What inspired **ACTION** will you take today?
What purposeful **CHANGE** will you make today?
What can you **TEACH** someone else today?

Happy Choosing Loving Thoughts that Energize and Uplift You!

Remember, nothing happens until you decide to take action!

Lead the Way Through Your BEING

"The way to gain a good reputation is to endeavor to be what you desire to appear."
~ Socrates

What a great quote! It reminds me of Gandhi's quote, "BE the change you seek in the world." I totally believe if we want to see purposeful change in our lives and in the world, we must endeavor to BE that which we seek. If you want to see more kindness, then BE more kind. If you want to see more love, then BE more loving. If you want to see more patience, then BE more patient. What purposeful change do you desire to see in your life and in the world? Once you answer that question, the next question becomes, then how do you BECOME more of that in your everyday life? By BEING more of what you seek, you create it! And others will see and notice it and be drawn to your leadership.

⁓ Empowered to A.C.T.: ⁓

What inspired **ACTION** will you take today?
What purposeful **CHANGE** will you make today?
What can you **TEACH** someone else today?

Happy BEING That Which You Desire to See in the World!

Remember, nothing happens until you decide to take action!

Do the People Around You Make You Happy?

"Take an honest inventory of your friends. Identify who makes you happy and spend more time with them."
~ Ralph Waldo Emerson

The people you spend your precious time and energy with is extremely important because it has the potential to impact you in a really big way; both for the good and the not so good! I meet with a powerful and select group of entrepreneurs each Friday morning for two hours. In those two hours a week I get a huge boost of energy, enthusiasm, and encouragement! I leave there wanting to be a better coach, speaker, business owner, and a better ME! On the contrary, if I watch 30 minutes of the news I find myself getting irritated, disgusted, and disappointed. I usually find myself wanting to complain about all the negativity happening in the world. How about you? How do the people around you impact you differently? Make a conscious choice to be around those who lift you up and energize you! And it may mean turning off the TV!

⁓ Empowered to A.C.T.: ⁓

What inspired **ACTION** will you take today?
What purposeful **CHANGE** will you make today?
What can you **TEACH** someone else today?

Happy Being Lifted Up and Energized!

Remember, nothing happens until you decide to take action!

Self-Growth is a Must!

"Very often a change of self is needed more than a change of scene."
~ Christopher Benson

Have you ever thought the grass was greener on the other side? I know I have and I've even gone over there to check it out! More often than not, the grass is NOT greener on the other side. It's usually the same ole grass, just on a different piece of land. Many times we are looking for happiness and brighter days in something outside of us. We think if we just change jobs, locations, spouses even, that we'll finally be happy. We think they are the problem and they need to change. Take a good look at your current circumstances and look for ways that YOU can change. Embrace your own self-growth. Look for ways that you can BE more!

— Empowered to A.C.T.: —

What inspired **ACTION** will you take today?
What purposeful **CHANGE** will you make today?
What can you **TEACH** someone else today?

Happy Embracing Your Self-Growth!

Remember, nothing happens until you decide to take action!

Let Go of Resistance

"The essence of any true transformation lies in the letting go."
~ Katherine Woodward Thomas

If you think about it, you ARE Superman or Superwoman! You just may not know it! You are stronger, more courageous, more beautiful, and more amazing than you think! Just yesterday I got caught in "thinking small" and a wonderful friend brought it to my attention and brought me back to my truth and to being the Superwoman that I am! It can be easy to forget sometimes, so be sure to flex your "greatness muscle" on a daily basis! Your greatness is your truth, you see. Don't deny the Superman or Superwoman inside of you from sharing and expressing your greatest gifts with others too. It's time to fly, my friend!

─◦ Empowered to A.C.T.: ◦─

What inspired **ACTION** will you take today?
What purposeful **CHANGE** will you make today?
What can you **TEACH** someone else today?

Happy Flying!

Remember, nothing happens until you decide to take action!

Are You Committed?

"Trade in the concept of staying motivated and replace it with commitment."
~ Jon Congdon

I am positive that everyone on this planet lacks motivation from time to time. It's natural and it's actually necessary to our evolution. Those moments when our commitment level is tested can actually turn into being life-altering moments! You have the chance to prove to yourself that no matter what happens, good, bad, or ugly, that you are committed to living in alignment to your purpose and to the creation of your vision. Think about a vision or goal you are working on right now and reignite your commitment to it! Affirm that you are in for the long haul!

⟿ Empowered to A.C.T.: ⟿

What inspired **ACTION** will you take today?
What purposeful **CHANGE** will you make today?
What can you **TEACH** someone else today?

Happy Being Committed to Your Purpose!

Remember, nothing happens until you decide to take action!

Think You Can't?

"You must do the things you think you cannot do."
~ Unknown

I love this quote. It really makes me stop and cause an interruption in my old stories that tell me I can't do something. It's just the "wake up call" I need to see a greater potential within me! Think about what stories you've been holding onto, the ones where you make excuses for why you haven't done something or created something you desire. It's time to start seeing those old deadbeat stories and glorified excuses are getting you nowhere! They are blocking you from living a more purposeful and fulfilled life! They are preventing you from serving those who need you most! Refuel your burning DESIRES! Reclaim your greatness and your potential today by doing the impossible!

⟶ Empowered to A.C.T.: ⟵

What inspired **ACTION** will you take today?
What purposeful **CHANGE** will you make today?
What can you **TEACH** someone else today?

Happy Doing What You Think You Cannot Do!

Remember, nothing happens until you decide to take action!

Step Into Your Courage!

"Courage is doing what you're afraid to do.
There can be no courage unless you're scared."
~ Eddie Rickenbacker

Are you wondering what to do about a particular situation? Maybe there is something you want to do but you've been putting it off for a long time now? Welcome to the quicksand of indecision. Without being able to make a sound decision to move forward and step into your true self and greatness, you stay stuck! Don't knock yourself down for being afraid to make a decision. The fear just means your current comfort zone is trying to protect you and keep you from stepping out. It's just doing its job. There is no courage without fear, so grab hold of some courage and pull yourself out of that nasty quicksand. Make a decision! Step up and step out and try something new. Take a risk and see what victory feels like.

⟶ Empowered to A.C.T.: ⟵

What inspired **ACTION** will you take today?
What purposeful **CHANGE** will you make today?
What can you **TEACH** someone else today?

Happy Courage!

Remember, nothing happens until you decide to take action!

Life is Waiting For You in The Moment

"Most people treat the present moment as if it were an obstacle that they need to overcome. Since the present moment is life itself, it is an insane way to live."
~ Eckhart Tolle

Do you ever find yourself working so hard to get "there" that you forget about "here?" Yup, me too! For most of us our upbringing and conditioning was not focused around being present and in the moment. Most of the time we're all thinking about "what's next" instead of "what's right here right now." We miss out on enjoying the moment and more importantly we miss out on enjoying LIFE. Set your intention to BE. HERE. NOW. That's where life is!

Empowered to A.C.T.:

What inspired **ACTION** will you take today?
What purposeful **CHANGE** will you make today?
What can you **TEACH** someone else today?

Happy Living Life In the Moment!

Remember, nothing happens until you decide to take action!

The World Belongs to You!

"The world beyond will not belong to 'managers' or those who can make the numbers dance. The world will belong to passionate, driven leaders—people who will not only have enormous amounts of energy but who can energize those whom they lead."
~ Jack Welch

The world has changed! No longer does the company who can manipulate the numbers best make it to the top. But rather, it's the company with the best leadership and culture that leaves the greatest mark and rises to the top. Those that have the drive and passion for making the world a better place and will stop at nothing to reach their dream are the ones who will out lead and out serve their competition as well as exceed the expectations of every customer! Is that you? Will you stop at nothing to reach for the moon? Go for it and bring everyone along with you!

— Empowered to A.C.T.: —

What inspired **ACTION** will you take today?
What purposeful **CHANGE** will you make today?
What can you **TEACH** someone else today?

Happy Making a Difference!

Remember, nothing happens until you decide to take action!

357

Everyone Deserves Respect and Gratitude!

"All businesses and jobs depend on a vast number of people, often unnoticed and unthanked, without which nothing really gets done. They are all human and deserve respect and gratitude."
~ Margaret Heffernan

This quote is so true! One of my pet peeves is when I see someone demoralizing or disrespecting someone who is serving them. It disgusts me actually. How has the world allowed this to happen? I believe it's our job, those with a higher conscious awareness, to create a shift in how service people are treated. And really it's not just service people, but anyone who is working an unnoticed and unthanked job. My call to action for you is to greet and thank every person you come across. Give them eye contact, smile, thank them for their service, and even go to the length of letting their manager know about a job well done. Imagine the amazing shift this will create in humanity! Everyone deserves respect and gratitude!

Empowered to A.C.T.:

What inspired **ACTION** will you take today?
What purposeful **CHANGE** will you make today?
What can you **TEACH** someone else today?

Happy Shifting Humanity Through Gratitude!

Remember, nothing happens until you decide to take action!

Smile Your Way to More Joy and Love!

"Let us always meet each other with smile,
for the smile is the beginning of love."
~ Mother Teresa

A smile is very inviting and a great way to connect with others. It can be one of the quickest and easiest ways to share some love with someone. I don't know about you, but when I have a smile on my face, my heart is usually smiling too. I have a greater sense of compassion, appreciation, and am more open. What about you? What does a smile do for you? How does it impact the experience you're having? Focus on smiling more today. Seek to share a smile with as many people as you can today. Then at the end of the day before you go to bed, notice how you feel. I'm going to guess that you'll feel much more joy and love! Yup, it's that simple to bring more joy and love into your life and into others' lives.

⊸ Empowered to A.C.T.: ⊶

What inspired **ACTION** will you take today?
What purposeful **CHANGE** will you make today?
What can you **TEACH** someone else today?

Happy Smiling Ear to Ear!

Remember, nothing happens until you decide to take action!

359

Give Thanks!

"Let us be grateful to people who make us happy; they are the
charming gardeners who make our souls blossom."
~ Marcel Proust

Give thanks today for those who positively impact your life. Make it extra special.
Express your gratitude and appreciation for them. I personally want to thank you
for allowing me to be a part of your everyday reading. I am honored to get a few
moments of your day to share some of my thoughts and passions. My intention is
that every day you will be inspired, energized, and empowered by these daily words
of wisdom. I hope they make a difference in how you show up in every area of your
life. Thank you!

⌐ Empowered to A.C.T.: ⌐

What inspired **ACTION** will you take today?
What purposeful **CHANGE** will you make today?
What can you **TEACH** someone else today?

Happy Thanksgiving!!

Remember, nothing happens until you decide to take action!

Be Led By Purpose

"To forget one's purpose is the commonest form of stupidity."
~ Friedrich Nietzsche

When you don't have a sense of purpose to your life and what you're really called to do, and then there will be a part of you that feels like you're aimlessly going through life—yeah, that's no fun! The reason why I think Nietzsche says it's the "commonest form of stupidity" is because first, unfortunately soooo many people are walking around unaware of their true purpose; second, it's stupid because YOU miss out on the greatest joy in life! I believe there is no greater fulfillment than to live a purpose-filled life! Be led by your purpose today. Ask yourself some great WHY and WHAT questions; why am I doing what I'm doing? What are my greater reasons? What will this give me? Why is this important to me?

Empowered to A.C.T.:

What inspired **ACTION** will you take today?
What purposeful **CHANGE** will you make today?
What can you **TEACH** someone else today?

Happy Being Led By Purpose!!

Remember, nothing happens until you decide to take action!

Get Used to it!

"Move out of your comfort zone. You can only grow if you are willing to feel awkward and uncomfortable when you try something new."
~ Brian Tracy

Remember when you were a child and you were comfortable with getting outside your comfort zone? It was almost as if you didn't know what a comfort zone was. You would fall and get up, fall and get up, and fall and get up again no matter how uncomfortable you got. As children, we keep our eye on the prize and we are persistent until we get it! So what happened? How come as adults we have such a fear of feeling awkward and uncomfortable that we will give up on our goals and dreams in a heartbeat! Well let's face it, as long as we have goals and dreams we are going to have to embrace and welcome the uncomfortable feeling! Why? Because if you never feel that awkward and uncomfortable feeling, then you are not growing! Uncomfortable feeling = Growth! Get used to it!

Empowered to A.C.T.:

What inspired **ACTION** will you take today?
What purposeful **CHANGE** will you make today?
What can you **TEACH** someone else today?

Happy Being Uncomfortable!!

Remember, nothing happens until you decide to take action!

December

Savor The "In-Between" Time

"I really believe that if you want to create something wonderful in your life, if you truly want to make a big change you've got to learn to tolerate the 'in-between' time. That's the period when we let go of who we know ourselves to be in order to allow for the possibility of who we might become."
~ Katherine Woodward Thomas

It can be difficult to be patient at times, can't it? You may decide you are ready to change and grow into a better version of yourself and then you want the results to be here yesterday! It can seem like an eternity before you see the physical results you desire. This "in-between" time as Katherine calls it, is the most critical time! It's the time you are letting go of the old and preparing to welcome the new. It's such a beautiful part of the process, however, most of us want nothing to do with it and we want the instant gratification of the results ASAP! I invite you to savor every moment of your journey and enjoy the ride. There's so much in store for you if you are patient and persistent through each phase of your becoming!

⁓ Empowered to A.C.T.: ⁓

What inspired **ACTION** will you take today?
What purposeful **CHANGE** will you make today?
What can you **TEACH** someone else today?

Happy Savoring the "In-Between" Time!!

Remember, nothing happens until you decide to take action!

You ARE Superman/ woman!

"What I do is based on powers we all have inside us; the ability to endure;
the ability to love; to carry on; to make the best of what we have—
and you don't have to be 'Superman' to do it."
~ Christopher Reeve

If you think about it, you ARE Superman or Superwoman! You just may not know it!
You are stronger, more courageous, more beautiful, and more amazing than you think! Just
yesterday I got caught in "thinking small" and a wonderful friend brought it to my attention
and brought me back to my truth and to being the Superwoman that I am! It can be easy to
forget sometimes, so be sure to flex your "greatness muscle" on a daily basis! Your greatness
is your truth, you see. Don't deny the Superman or Superwoman inside of you from sharing
and expressing your greatest gifts with others too. It's time to fly, my friend!

⸺ Empowered to A.C.T.: ⸺

What inspired **ACTION** will you take today?
What purposeful **CHANGE** will you make today?
What can you **TEACH** someone else today?

Happy Flying!

Remember, nothing happens until you decide to take action!

Today's Featured Reader:
Micki Spors, Rochester, Minnesota
"This is one my personal favorites! So often as women we feel challenged to be Superwoman!
This message reminds me that I already am SUPER! We all have greatness and 'super' inside of
us. It's good to be reminded, so I have this W.O.W. saved so I can reference it regularly! Thanks!"

Give, Give, Give and Receive, Receive, Receive

"What is so interesting about giving is not only that it pays, but that it pays in such unexpected ways. When you live with generosity, blessings come to you from corners and avenues you never would have expected."

~ Bob Burg

It's not our job to determine when, where, how, or from whom our receiving will come from. It comes from all places and people and many times it's from unexpected places and people! Don't you just love when something or someone comes into your life that's beyond your wildest dreams? Be careful not to shut the door to your receiving by only looking for it to come from one place. There is actually no limit to the amount of your receiving! The possibilities truly are endless! I invite you to give, give, give and serve the best you know how and just be open, open, open to receiving from all corners. There are no limits!

⁓ Empowered to A.C.T.: ⁓

What inspired **ACTION** will you take today?
What purposeful **CHANGE** will you make today?
What can you **TEACH** someone else today?

Happy Giving and Receiving From All Corners!

Remember, nothing happens until you decide to take action!

Welcome the Possibilities!

"Your true potential will speak as loud as your willingness to listen will allow it. If you simply breathe for the next 365 days, your life is going to be different, but is that the 'different' you want to create in your life? You have to make your possibilities welcome in your life."
~ Mary Morrissey

Mary Morrissey has a way of saying things that really hit me at my core. When you take a look at your life, there may be parts of it you would like to change. However, in order for that change to become your reality, you must believe in your potential to change it as well as welcome and "make room" for it to come into your life. If not, the change won't happen. You see, if are you not willing to listen to the creative power within you, you will block yourself from "hearing" and "seeing" a greater potential in yourself. Declare today that you are open, ready, and willing to receive greater clarity on your potential and your possibilities!

— Empowered to A.C.T.: —

What inspired **ACTION** will you take today?
What purposeful **CHANGE** will you make today?
What can you **TEACH** someone else today?

Happy Potential and Possibilities!

Remember, nothing happens until you decide to take action!

Comfort Zone City Isn't so Comfortable!

"You have to leave the city of your comfort and go into the wilderness of your intuition. What you'll discover will be wonderful. What you'll discover is yourself."
~ Alan Alda

Staying in "comfort zone city" sure seems easy, doesn't it? However, if you really think about it, when we neglect to leave our comfort zones, we are actually denying ourselves our true nature and those things we really want. We suppress, avoid, and ignore our true selves. That doesn't feel good at all! So the question is, is staying in that city really all that easy? What if you ventured out into the wilderness of your authentic self? Imagine what you could find. Wow! There's something special there and you'll never find it on the so called easy "comfort zone city." I challenge you to take a new perspective. It's the road less traveled that reaps great rewards and that feels absolutely amazing! The only thing making it difficult is your thought process. Trust yourself and your decisions and you'll feel stronger than ever!

⟶ Empowered to A.C.T.: ⟵

What inspired **ACTION** will you take today?
What purposeful **CHANGE** will you make today?
What can you **TEACH** someone else today?

Happy Finding Your Authentic Self!

Remember, nothing happens until you decide to take action!

Maximize the Purpose of This Moment!

"There is surely nothing other than the single purpose of the present moment. A man's whole life is a succession of moment after moment. If one fully understands the present moment, there will be nothing else to do, and nothing else to pursue. Live being true to the single purpose of the moment."
~ Yamamoto Tsunetomo

This very moment has tremendous purpose and so does the next moment and the next moment and so on. When we acknowledge the great purpose each moment bears, we seek ways to maximize and fulfill more of our purpose and the potential of that moment. When we believe a moment is just a moment and are just anxious to make it to the end of the day, we miss out on living with greater purpose and ultimately fulfilling our potential. What a waste of purpose and potential! Starting NOW, never miss out on the chance to be present, right here right now, and make more of this moment than you ever imagined possible!

⟶ Empowered to A.C.T.: ⟵

What inspired **ACTION** will you take today?
What purposeful **CHANGE** will you make today?
What can you **TEACH** someone else today?

Happy Maximizing Each Moment!

Remember, nothing happens until you decide to take action!

Go For IT!

"Things are only impossible until they're not."
~ Unknown

Someone once told the Wright brothers that it was impossible to fly. Someone once said it was impossible to put a man on the moon. I'm sure someone has also told you that something you desire is impossible. Decide here and now what you are going to is possible and impossible in your life. I challenge you to fuel your beliefs around your dreams and desires. Your greatest dreams and desires await you and there's no time to stand around listening to those naysayers who are afraid to fly. Spread your wings and go for it. Turn your "impossibilities" into reality and step forward toward your dreams today.

Empowered to A.C.T.:

What inspired **ACTION** will you take today?
What purposeful **CHANGE** will you make today?
What can you **TEACH** someone else today?

Happy Going For Your Dreams!

Remember, nothing happens until you decide to take action!

Be a Change Agent With Gratitude

"A smart manager will establish a culture of gratitude. Expand the appreciative attitude to suppliers, vendors, delivery people, and of course, customers."
~ Harvey Mackay

Having a culture of gratitude and appreciation is a smart way of doing business, a way of operating. It becomes the way in which you communicate with everyone in your organization as well as outside your organization. What a beautiful thing! We could use more organizations like this, don't you say?! Whether you run your own business, manage a team, or work on a team, think about how you can be a change agent. How can you begin to instill a culture of gratitude and appreciation? Maybe there's a co-worker of yours who helped you out with a project, helped you solve a problem, or who's done a really great job on their own projects, take a moment to acknowledge them and express your thanks. Commit to do this every day. Be patient, stick with it and watch the culture begin to shift. The more influence you have in an organization, the more quickly you'll see things begin to shift.

⌁ Empowered to A.C.T.: ⌁

What inspired **ACTION** will you take today?
What purposeful **CHANGE** will you make today?
What can you **TEACH** someone else today?

Happy Culture of Gratitude!

Remember, nothing happens until you decide to take action!

Love is a necessity, Not an Option!

"A flower cannot blossom without sunshine,
and man cannot live without love."
~ Max Muller

Love is one of our human needs. We all need it. Just like a flower dies without sunshine, humans die without love. A human may still have a heartbeat and pulse, but they are empty and dead inside. Unfortunately this is when people may turn to destructive behaviors in order to seek love. It's not healthy and by no means is it serving our higher purpose. Think about ways to pour more love into the lives of others as well as open up and receive more love into your own life. Get all the sunshine and water you can so you can blossom in a healthy and beautiful way!

—⁓ Empowered to A.C.T.: ⁓—

What inspired **ACTION** will you take today?
What purposeful **CHANGE** will you make today?
What can you **TEACH** someone else today?

Happy Blossoming!

Remember, nothing happens until you decide to take action!

Think Differently, Do Differently

"There's plenty of intelligence in the world, but the courage to do things differently is in short supply."
~ Marilyn Vos Savant

I love that this world is full of highly intelligent people who love to learn and grow and have tons of life experience to share. However, with that said, it breaks my heart to know that a ton of these same people are just conforming to the crowd and not following their dreams and what's in their heart. When you begin to think outside the box for yourself, you welcome a whole new level of living into your life. The motto for my company Xtreme Results is, "Helping you THINK differently so you can DO differently." Be willing to break free from your normal thought process today and think a little differently. And the more you do, the more you will find yourself doing things differently, which will ultimately creates new results in your life! Your greatness is awaiting you!

⌐ Empowered to A.C.T.: ⌐

What inspired **ACTION** will you take today?
What purposeful **CHANGE** will you make today?
What can you **TEACH** someone else today?

Happy Thinking and Doing Differently!

Remember, nothing happens until you decide to take action!

Stay True to Your Purpose

"True happiness ... is not attained through self-gratification,
but through fidelity to a worthy purpose."
~ Helen Keller

Purpose gives your life a greater meaning. It makes getting out of bed so much more fun and worth it! When you are truly YOU ... no pretending, no perfectionism, no "trying so hard," but rather YOU being YOU making purposeful decisions in your life, you will experience a whole other level of happiness! We all get busy and pulled in many directions, but this is something you don't want to stray from or neglect, but rather you want to make it the center of your life. Make your purpose be the reason why you do anything and everything! Stay true to your purpose and you'll be happy you did!

⌐ Empowered to A.C.T.: ⌐

What inspired **ACTION** will you take today?
What purposeful **CHANGE** will you make today?
What can you **TEACH** someone else today?

Happy Being True to Your Purpose!

Remember, nothing happens until you decide to take action!

Don't Give Into the Temptation of Giving Up!

"The most common trait I have found in all successful people is that they have conquered the temptation to give up."
~ Peter Lowe

Giving up sure can look tempting at times, can't it? You may talk yourself into thinking it's just easier to give up. In that moment it may seem like the easier choice, however long term, it actually just makes things harder for you. Successful people have trained themselves to be connected to their vision and purpose at all times. When decision time comes, they are able to make choices that are in alignment to their ultimate calling no matter how difficult the choice may be. Giving up is just a disconnect from your vision and purpose! Don't give up, just reconnect to your heart and soul and see your greatest vision and purpose and let that fuel drive you forward!

⁓ Empowered to A.C.T.: ⁓

What inspired **ACTION** will you take today?
What purposeful **CHANGE** will you make today?
What can you **TEACH** someone else today?

Happy Not Giving Up!

Remember, nothing happens until you decide to take action!

Got Confidence?

"Just why do you need confidence in yourself? First of all, it will give you stability in every area of your life. Confidence equals contentment with self; contentment is knowing you have all you need for the present circumstances."
~ John C. Maxwell

Have you ever been in a situation where you felt you had little to no confidence and low self-esteem? I'm sure we've all been there before at one time or another. Actually, many people may be feeling that way right now. There may be a part of you that doesn't see your magnificence and greatness and therefore doesn't fully believe you are capable of creating amazing things. That limiting belief will always stifle your confidence in thinking that you are fully resourced, right here, right now. When you are confident, you will know with certainty that you are fully capable of create amazing things and you won't question it. Don't rob yourself of the wonderful feeling of confidence! Take 5 minutes today to reflect on the great gifts and talents you have been given. Find confidence in knowing that they will help you with whatever situation and project you are currently dealing with today.

— Empowered to A.C.T.: —

What inspired **ACTION** will you take today?
What purposeful **CHANGE** will you make today?
What can you **TEACH** someone else today?

Happy Confident YOU!

Remember, nothing happens until you decide to take action!

Live Your Greatness

"Your time is limited, so don't waste it living someone else's life. Don't be trapped by dogma—which is living with the results of other people's thinking. Don't let the noise of others' opinions drown out your own inner voice. And most important, have the courage to follow your heart and intuition. They somehow already know what you truly want to become. Everything else is secondary."
~ Steve Jobs

Whose life are you living? Yours or someone else's? I say this with love— YOUR DAYS ARE NUMBERED! Nobody really knows when their time is up here on this beautiful planet of ours, so why settle for anything less than your true greatness. Now is the time to live YOUR life! Express the purpose that lives in YOUR heart, reach YOUR cherished aspirations, and be willing to face YOUR fears. Realize you are not reading this message by accident. You are reading it for a reason. You have greatness within you. It's time to live your greatness! Yes, right here, right now!

～ Empowered to A.C.T.: ～

What inspired **ACTION** will you take today?
What purposeful **CHANGE** will you make today?
What can you **TEACH** someone else today?

Happy Living YOUR Greatness!

Remember, nothing happens until you decide to take action!

Green Lights All the Way!

"Problems are just green lights to keep going, not stop signs."
~ David Argo

I love that, your problems are NOT stop signs! They're not a reason to quit! We all have problems and if we all looked at problems as stop signs we'd all be sitting here doing nothing! Instead choose to see problems as a green light to keep going and find a way to be resourceful and come out ahead! Next time you are faced with a problem, see it as a green light and forge forward instead of seeing it as a reason to stop. Dig deep and brainstorm ideas, options, solutions, answers, and don't stop until you come up with something that you can take action on.

‿ Empowered to A.C.T.: ‿

What inspired **ACTION** will you take today?
What purposeful **CHANGE** will you make today?
What can you **TEACH** someone else today?

Happy Green Lights!

Remember, nothing happens until you decide to take action!

Are You Afraid of a Challenge?

"It's lack of faith that makes people afraid of meeting
challenges, and I believed in myself."
~ Muhammad Ali

Do you ever shy away from a challenge? Maybe you find yourself not even putting
yourself out there to even be challenged in the first place! Hmmm ... why is that?
There may be many variables to the situation, but beneath it all, there is a lack of
faith and belief. Instead of starting a challenge off with focusing on all the complex
variables, how about start with affirming your belief and faith in yourself?! One
hundred percent of the challenge starts in your head! Your heart knows the truth!
Your heart knows how amazing you are! So work on getting out of your head
and into your heart. Affirm your faith and belief in yourself. Feel it in your heart
and the challenge will nearly be won! Then use your mind to work through the
variables. Are you up for the challenge? Prove it! Go give today your ALL!

⁓ Empowered to A.C.T.: ⁓

What inspired **ACTION** will you take today?
What purposeful **CHANGE** will you make today?
What can you **TEACH** someone else today?

Happy Challenges!

Remember, nothing happens until you decide to take action!

Rejuvenate!

"In dealing with those who are undergoing great suffering, if you feel 'burnout' setting in, if you feel demoralized and exhausted, it is best, for the sake of everyone, to restore yourself. The point is to have a long-term perspective."
~ Dalai Lama

Life happens and sometimes those things that come and go don't always feel good. But really, it's how we perceive those things that creates the pain in our lives. It's our mind that creates the worry, grief or suffering. So if you are suffering from burnout or exhaustion right now, it's time to let go, nurture yourself and come back to your CENTER. Connect with your higher self, align with your God. See the long term perspective, because the tide ALWAYS comes back in. ALWAYS.

Empowered to A.C.T.:

What inspired **ACTION** will you take today?
What purposeful **CHANGE** will you make today?
What can you **TEACH** someone else today?

Happy Rejuvenating Yourself!

Remember, nothing happens until you decide to take action!

Be Still. Be Present.

"I know that the purpose of life is to understand and be in the present moment with the people you love. It's just that simple."
~ Jane Seymour

We like to make life a whole lot more complicated than it really needs to be, don't we?! What if we just dwelled in the experience this moment has to offer? What do you think you would come to learn and understand about life and those you care most about if you were more present? When we're present it's as if we are wearing a new pair of glasses and we see the world in a whole different way. Be still. Be present. What do you notice? Notice what you notice when you're present. Do this when you're with your loved ones too. It's amazing to see what you notice when you are present in your most cherished relationships!

─◦ Empowered to A.C.T.: ◦─

What inspired **ACTION** will you take today?
What purposeful **CHANGE** will you make today?
What can you **TEACH** someone else today?

Happy Noticing What You Notice!

Remember, nothing happens until you decide to take action!

Go Climb a Mountain!

"Stop talking to God about how big your mountains are, and start talking to your mountains about how big your God is."
~ Joel Osteen

We all have obstacles that cross our paths from time to time, some bigger than others. Isn't it interesting how these obstacles always seem to come at the most inopportune moments too? If you spend time dwelling on how big or how many obstacles you face, then you are drowning yourself in self-pity and sending out an energy and attitude of "poor me." That, my friend, will get you nowhere. I'm challenging you here and now to trust, to have faith. Let go of the worry, fear or doubt. They are only keeping you stuck at the base of the mountain. Know who walks beside you. With pure faith, you can **MOVE** any mountain. Believe in yourself and the power of your dreams and burning desires. With your God, you are bigger than any mountain. Now go climb one!

Empowered to A.C.T.:

What inspired **ACTION** will you take today?
What purposeful **CHANGE** will you make today?
What can you **TEACH** someone else today?

Happy Climbing Mountains!

Remember, nothing happens until you decide to take action!

Give Thanks For the "Ordinary"

"I don't have to chase extraordinary moments to find happiness—it's right in front of me if I'm paying attention and practicing gratitude."
~ Brene Brown

When you make practicing gratitude a part of your everyday life, you'll have no problem finding happiness in every and all "ordinary" moments. Look around and find the "extra" ordinary in the ordinary. Notice and give thanks for the brightness of the colors around you, take in the scent of your environment, savor the flavors in your mouth, listen for what you normally ignore, feel the different textures on your skin. Next time you are feeling unimpressed with happiness level of your day, try practicing gratitude and see what unfolds.

⁓ Empowered to A.C.T.: ⁓

What inspired **ACTION** will you take today?
What purposeful **CHANGE** will you make today?
What can you **TEACH** someone else today?

Happy Practicing Gratitude With the "Ordinary!"

Remember, nothing happens until you decide to take action!

Be Guided By Your Heart

"Sometimes the heart sees what is invisible to the eye."
~ H. Jackson Brown, Jr.

Do you ever sometimes find yourself trying to make logical sense out of that which you love? And then maybe you put rules around what you "should" and "shouldn't" love and before you know it you have a rule book on who, what, when, and how you are supposed to love? I know I have at times. I'll be soooo in my head trying to make sense of everything instead of getting into my heart and feeling it out and trusting it. You see, there are many times you may find love, compassion, and appreciation in your heart for something that doesn't make sense. Or I'll be drawn to someone or something and I won't necessarily understand why. I've come to learn to trust my feelings more and be guided by my heart. On the surface I may not see it, but my heart does! Let your heart be your eyes!

⟶ Empowered to A.C.T.: ⟵

What inspired **ACTION** will you take today?
What purposeful **CHANGE** will you make today?
What can you **TEACH** someone else today?

Happy Letting Your Heart Be Your Eyes!

Remember, nothing happens until you decide to take action!

What Experience Will You Create Today

"What you choose to put your focus on
will determine the experience you have."
~ Kelly Sylte

What have you chosen to focus your thoughts on and put your energy into today? Success or struggle? Freedom or stress? The thoughts we choose influence the experience we have in every moment. I found myself feeling overwhelmed last week and I caught myself red-handed creating the overwhelming experience with my thoughts! I was actually feeding the overwhelm with thoughts and feelings of being in over my head! I quickly chose a new thought pattern ... one that served me better. One that calmed me and brought me the power of the present moment. I was then able to choose more purposeful thoughts, which completely changed the experience I was having! What experience will you create today?

⤙ Empowered to A.C.T.: ⤚

What inspired **ACTION** will you take today?
What purposeful **CHANGE** will you make today?
What can you **TEACH** someone else today?

Happy Thoughts!

Remember, nothing happens until you decide to take action!

Are You Drained or Energized?

"Don't be weighed down by things that drain your energy! If it doesn't bring you joy chuck it, change it, or rearrange it!"
~ Ralph Waldo Emerson

Great questions I like to ask myself frequently about the things I do, places I go, and people I hang out with are, "Am I lifted up or drained ... Am I energized or dragged down ... Am I inspired or frustrated?" The answers to these questions really help me make decisions as to where and with whom I spend my time. You never get a minute back ... the power is always in this present moment. Choose to be in environments and around people who lift you up, energize you, and inspire you! Just by making this a part of your decision making process, you will open yourself up to receiving greater energy, joy and bliss into your life!

Empowered to A.C.T.:

What inspired **ACTION** will you take today?
What purposeful **CHANGE** will you make today?
What can you **TEACH** someone else today?

Happy Being Lifted Up, Energized, and Inspired!

Remember, nothing happens until you decide to take action!

The Law of Environment

"The Law of the Environment: Growth thrives in conducive surroundings."
~ John C. Maxwell

This is the law that requires you to take a look around and ask yourself some very important questions. Such as, "WHO are you hanging around with?" and "WHERE are you hanging out?" If you are honest with yourself, you know that in five years you will be the product of who you hang around with and where you are spending your time. The answers are right in front of you! Make the choice to surround yourself with people who make you want to be a better you. Spend your time at places that lift you up, inspire and energize you. Your growth and success depends on it!

Empowered to A.C.T.:

What inspired **ACTION** will you take today?
What purposeful **CHANGE** will you make today?
What can you **TEACH** someone else today?

Happy Conducive Environments!

Remember, nothing happens until you decide to take action!

Your Purpose is a Journey

"Your Purpose is a Journey, Not an Event."
~ Unknown

What a beautiful quote! Your purpose is not a destination, nor is it something with an end date. Your purpose is something that drives and guides you every day, all day, until your last day. Don't look for the finished result, but rather enjoy every step of the journey. Look for how every step comes packed with great meaning and fulfillment! With that said, slow down a little bit and enjoy the ride. Stop to smell the roses, smile, and appreciate all the purpose in the moment right here right now. You'll experience every moment differently if you do! Enjoy them!

⌐ Empowered to A.C.T.: ⌐

What inspired **ACTION** will you take today?
What purposeful **CHANGE** will you make today?
What can you **TEACH** someone else today?

Happy Purposeful Moments!

Remember, nothing happens until you decide to take action!

Be an Example of Excellence

*"Great spirits have always encountered violent
Opposition from mediocre minds."*
~ Albert Einstein

Have you ever noticed how small minded people are quick to shoot down an idea or be a naysayer in your life? It is very easy for them to do so because they are operating from a mediocre mentality and when they see you doing something that displays excellence they don't resonate with it, so then they therefore shoot it down. No need to take it personally or get upset by this, even though I know that's easier said than done, but rather see it for what it is. Just know that person doesn't have the same level of thinking as you do. Keep forging forward with your big thinking and let your excellence and greatness ooze right of you and create something beyond your wildest dreams!

Empowered to A.C.T.:

What inspired **ACTION** will you take today?
What purposeful **CHANGE** will you make today?
What can you **TEACH** someone else today?

Happy Displaying Excellence!

Remember, nothing happens until you decide to take action!

Get Those Feet Moving!

"Dreams come true, all they need is you."
~ Mike Dooley

You are the person who has to decide. Will you do it? Will you reach for your dreams or will you sit on the sidelines and just watch life pass you by? It takes action to move forward in any venture. Here's an exercise. Stand in place ... look ahead in the distance. I don't care if you look 10 feet ahead or 100 yards, just look ahead. Now try to get there without moving. Hmmm? Get anywhere? I didn't think so. Your dreams require the same action. They require you to move forward, no one else can do it for you. You must have movement. You must step forward to move forward. Can you see your dreams there off in the distance? They're all yours, my friend. Now get moving and go get them!

⌐ Empowered to A.C.T.: ⌐

What inspired **ACTION** will you take today?
What purposeful **CHANGE** will you make today?
What can you **TEACH** someone else today?

Happy Taking Forward Moving Action!

Remember, nothing happens until you decide to take action!

Build an Estimate Full of Possibility!

"If you are distressed by anything external, the pain is not due to the thing itself, but to your estimate of it; and this you have the power to revoke at any moment."
~ Marcus Aurelius

We have a tendency to make mountains out of molehills. We create all these scenarios in our minds of the bad things that "could" happen. Well, what if it doesn't happen that way? What if, in fact, something really great and amazing happens? Now that's what I'm talking about! Don't waste your brain power saturated in fear, worry or doubt. Spend your time thinking of all the possibilities and opportunities and watch the magic happen. If you have given yourself an estimate that includes pain, revoke it right now. Submit an estimate of what you really want and start building on that!

— Empowered to A.C.T.: —

What inspired **ACTION** will you take today?
What purposeful **CHANGE** will you make today?
What can you **TEACH** someone else today?

Happy Building Possibilities!

Remember, nothing happens until you decide to take action!

Live Your Dream!

"Don't worry about all the other stuff or all the other people.
Just focus on you and what you can do to make this year special.
Focus on what you can do to take yourself to a new level."
~ Unknown

It literally breaks my heart to see how many dreams are wasted because people choose to spend their time worrying about what someone else is or isn't doing. What does that have to do with you accomplishing your dream? Dreams are also often abandoned because of what someone else says or thinks about them. Again, what does that have to do with you accomplishing your dream? Don't let those people steal your dreams. Misery loves company and they are inviting you into their misery with their rhetoric. Stay focused on YOU. Nurture yourself, BE YOU, and honor your dreams. Take yourself to a new level and you'll find yourself high above their junk. This is your opportunity to make next year special.

⟿ Empowered to A.C.T.: ⟿

What inspired **ACTION** will you take today?
What purposeful **CHANGE** will you make today?
What can you **TEACH** someone else today?

Happy Going to a Whole New Level!

Remember, nothing happens until you decide to take action!

Your Mind is Your Workshop

"You can build things with your mind, not only your hands!"
~ Steve Sitkowski

Your mind is your workshop. Once you are gifted with an idea, your mind is intended to be the place where the development of that idea begins. All things created by humans begin as just a thought, just an idea in their imagination. Therefore, everything is created twice, first in the human mind in our imagination and second in the physical form. It isn't until you take your idea beyond your mind and your imagination, that it has a chance to come alive in the physical form. You can't just develop your idea in your mind; you must also take the necessary inspired action steps to create it in the physical form—that's when you get your hands involved! What ideas do you need to take some inspired action on? Let's roll up those sleeves and get our hands dirty!

⟶ Empowered to A.C.T.: ⟵

What inspired **ACTION** will you take today?
What purposeful **CHANGE** will you make today?
What can you **TEACH** someone else today?

Happy Building Ideas With Your Mind AND Your Hands!

Remember, nothing happens until you decide to take action!

Give With a BIG Heart and Receive With An Open Heart

"All the giving in the world won't bring success, won't create the results you want, unless you make yourself willing and able to receive in like measure. The Law of Receptivity: The key to effective giving is to stay open to receiving."
~ Bob Burg

Why is it that giving seems so easy but the receiving is just so darn right difficult? What if it wasn't? You see, we've been conditioned to think that way. We've been taught that "it is better to give than to receive." Now don't get me wrong. Giving is important and it is great to give, but you can't leave out the receiving part. In Bob Burg's book, *The Go Giver*, he talks about how giving and receiving is very much like breathing. Which would you say is more important, breathing IN or breathing OUT? Hmmmm? Guess what. They are equally important to sustain life, aren't they? You must breathe in before you can breathe out and vise versa. Giving and receiving works the same way. If you want to give effectively, you MUST be willing to receiving without shame, guilt or a need to pay back. The receiving fills your cup so that you have more to give. Allow it. Welcome it. Call for it and share the harvest.

⟶ Empowered to A.C.T.: ⟵

What inspired **ACTION** will you take today?
What purposeful **CHANGE** will you make today?
What can you **TEACH** someone else today?

Happy Receiving!

Remember, nothing happens until you decide to take action!

A Special Closing Story to Keep You Energized, Inspired, and Empowered!

The Law of the Garbage Truck

One day I hopped in a taxi and we took off for the airport. We were driving in the right lane when suddenly a black car jumped out of the parking space right in front of us. My taxi driver slammed on his breaks, skidded, and missed the other car by just inches! The driver of the other car whipped his head around and started yelling at us. My taxi driver just smiled and waved at the guy. So I asked, "Why did you just do that? This guy almost caused an accident and sent us to the hospital!" This is when my taxi driver taught me what I now call, "The Law of the Garbage Truck."

He explained that many people are like garbage trucks. They run around full of garbage, full of frustration, full of anger, full of disappointment and rage. As their garbage piles up, they need a place to dump it and sometimes they'll dump it on you. Don't take it personally. Just smile, wave, wish them well, and move on. Don't pick up their garbage and spread it to other people in your life, whether at work, at home, or to people that you don't even know on the streets.

Always remember that good people do not let garbage trucks take over their day. Life is too short to wake up in the morning with regrets, so ... "Love the people who treat you right and forgive and pray for the ones who don't."

Today's Featured Readers:
Stephanie Bohr Crane, Kenosha, Wisconsin
"My absolute favorite Daily W.O.W. is the Law of the Garbage Truck! I have seen how negativity breeds negativity and I made a decision a long time ago not to reproduce it. This W.O.W. has impacted my life because it is a reminder to not sweat the small stuff, but realize everything is small stuff. However, each person has to make up one's mind on how to react it. I believe I have taught this to each person I have managed in the last 10 years, and hopefully am passing this same skill to my 6-year-old son. Thank you for all you do, Melissa."

Tina Balaka, Greenfield, Wisconsin
"I really love the story about the Law of the Garbage Truck! It has helped me to not take on the problems of someone else and don't let the bad day someone else is having affect my day. Particularly when I'm working with clients I can easily take on their problems as my own and I can choose to take their baggage with me for the day or not. While I certainly want to be a problem solver for my clients and provide them with service I also don't want to let their problems become of prime of my day. I want to address the problem or situation, come to a decision, and move on. Thanks, Melissa!"

Conclusion:

DON'T START YOUR DAY WITHOUT IT!

Congratulations. You've completed your W.O.W. journey and discovered more energy, inspiration, and empowerment within the process. You're well on your way to create an even more amazing life for yourself and others.

Don't move on too quickly though. Just because you've "finished" reading the book doesn't mean you're done just yet. Remember, success begins with the way you start your day.

This book isn't meant to be read just once. Instead it's meant to be read year after year. It's also meant to be passed onto friends who need a little energy infused into their lives.

Next time we chat, I hope it will be at a live event where we'll both be shaking our tambourines or *Your Daily W.O.W.* books, if you prefer.

Until that time,

Melissa West

ABOUT THE AUTHOR

Melissa West (Malueg) is the founder and CEO of Xtreme Results, LLC—a powerful catalyst for life transformation. She encourages business professionals to rediscover their passion and empowers them to create the amazing life of their dreams. She shares this message worldwide through coaching, training, mentoring, and keynote speaking.

In 2011, Melissa became business partners with John C. Maxwell—the #1 leadership guru in the world. Today she serves as a faculty member for his certification program. As part of this elite international team of 6, she has helped over 3,200 professionals from more than 101 countries build their own coaching, speaking, and training businesses.

Melissa holds a bachelor's degree in Management Information Systems from the University of Wisconsin-Milwaukee and is a graduate from the Institute for Professional Excellence in Coaching (IPEC) where she earned her Certified as a Professional Coach and Energy Leadership Index Master Practitioner accreditations.

Melissa lives with her husband Chris in North Carolina. Connect with her at XtremeResultsCoaching.com

XtremeRESULTS | Think differently. Do differently.

DAILY *Words of Wisdom*

"Rather than depleting yourself with judgments about what you haven't done, who you could have become, why you haven't moved faster, or what you should have changed, re-direct that energy toward the next big push -- the one that takes you from good enough to better. The one that takes you from adequate to extraordinary. The one that helps you rise up from a low moment and helps you reach your personal best." ~ Oprah Winfrey

---

What amazing words! How can you look at this present moment, right now, as an opportunity to redirect your energy toward your next big success? You start from where you are — that's your starting point. Forget the coulda, woulda, shouldas... Start NOW. Be PRESENT and give today your personal best! Happy Personal Best! ~ Melissa West

---

Ready to be inspired, energized, and empowered every day? Visit XtremeResultsCoaching.com and register to receive your free "Daily Words of Widsom" today!

Melissa West I Melissa@XtremeResultsCoaching.com I 414-243-3661

www.XtremeResultsCoaching.com